THE DOWSING MIND

THE DOWSING MIND

Into the Multi-Dimensional Realms and Back

Gary White

To Elyn Aviva, my fellow imaginaut and dearest life companion

The Dowsing Mind

Into the Multi-Dimensional Realms and Back

by

Gary White

Copyright © 2020 by Pilgrims Process Publishers

http://www.PowerfulPlaces.com

http://PilgrimsProcess.com

All rights reserved. No part of this publication, including illustrations, may be reproduced in any form or by any means, electronic or mechanical, including photocopy, recording, or any information storage and retrieval system, without permission in writing from the publisher.

Disclaimer: Nothing in this book is intended to diagnose or treat any health condition. Follow any instructions or techniques at your own risk. Please consult your health care professional for any medical advice.

ISBN: 978-0-9915267-7-2

Set in Minon Pro 11 pt. and Salden Black in various sizes.

Photo Credits: Gary White, Elyn Aviva, and Adobe Stock

Contents

Introduction   1
Part One   5
   What Is Dowsing?   5
   Why Dowse? 5
   Tangible and Intangible Dowsing   6
   Dowsing Devices   6
   The Dowsing Mind   7
   Left Brain vs Right Brain   8
   Neural Oscillations   9
   Harmonizing with Your Surroundings   9
   Asking Permission   10
   Experiment #1: Pausing the Left Brain   10
   Why Do We Need to Pause the Left Brain?   11
   What Are These Multi-Dimensional Realms?   11
   Experiment #2: Stillness Meditation   12
   Experiment #3: Practicing with a Pendulum   13
   But I Can Make the Pendulum Do Anything I Want It To!   17
   What Is Going on Here?   17
   Experiment #4: L-shaped Rods   18
   Dowsing with a Purpose   23
   Dowsing for Information   24
   Visualization   24
   Experiment #5: Another L-rod Exercise   26
   Getting It Set in Your System   27
   Practical Dowsing   28

What's Really Going on 28

Faery Magic 30

Dowsing for Lines 31

Intention 31

Experiment #6: Dowsing for a Piece of Yarn 32

Grounding Techniques 33

Fault Lines 33

Experiment #7: Fault Lines 34

Experiment #8: Discovering the Orientation of a Fault 35

Dowsing for More 36

Story Time Again 38

Further Information about Dowsing Tools 40

Do Those Fancy Devices Work? 45

SAAMA, an Example in the Realm of Health 46

Filters 47

Dowsing in the Supermarket 48

Experiment #9: Muscle Testing 49

Experiment #10: And Now the Supermarket 50

Expanding Beyond the Supermarket 55

And Now, Dowsing for Life 56

A Walkabout in the USA 56

Asking Questions Precisely 60

Determining Proper Dosage 62

Dowsing for the Depth of Water 63

It's Practice Time 63

The Next Part of Our Elen of the Ways Adventure 64

Summary 67

Part Two   69

   How I Discovered the Multi-Dimensional Realms 69

   Where Is the Multi-Dimensional World?   74

   Time in Multi-Dimensional Space   75

   The Multi-Dimensional Realms and Dowsing 76

   A Deeper Dive into Dowsing 77

   Prelude to Multi-Dimensional Sight   78

   Multi-Dimensional Sight   80

   Extrasensory Perception   81

   Story Time 81

   Frequencies of Reality   83

   "Going Multi-Dimensional" 84

   Experiment #11: X-ray Vision   84

   Experiment #12: Another Hypnogogic Exercise   85

   Experiment #13: A Meditation Exercise   86

   Experiment #14: A Night-Time Dream Practice 86

   Gentle Warning   87

   But Is It Safe out There?   87

Part Three   89

   Even Deeper 89

   An Appeal to Conscience   90

   Resonance   90

   Experiment #15: Tuning the Instrument   91

   Harmonizing on a Grand Scale: The Walkabout 92

   Experiment #16: Experiencing a Walkabout   96

   The Prevailing Fantasy   98

Part Four   99

The Problem of Consciousness 99

Subjective Space – Map Dowsing   100

Dowsing for Health   102

Subjective Time   102

Does All Matter Have Consciousness? 103

Experiment #17: Making Friends with Plants and Stones   104

The Scope of the Multi-Dimensional Realms   107

A Spiritual Practice   107

Bringing It Back to the 3-D Realm   109

Conclusion   111

Additional Resources   113

   National Dowsing Societies   113

   Bibliography 114

   Links   115

Index   117

About the Author   121

Introduction

Our ancient ancestors lived completely different lives from ours. They stood on the ground by day and looked at the sky at night. This gave them a sense of connection to the Earth that most of us generally miss. Most Westerners stand on floors all day and seldom see the starlit sky at night because of light pollution.

Our ancient ancestors also had very different needs from ours. For example, they needed to be able to find drinkable water that didn't show on the surface of the land. If you grew up as I did, as a middle-class kid in the midwest of the USA, you probably simply walked to the kitchen sink and turned on the tap for an unending supply of potable water. We had no need to be able to find that blind spring or deep-water source hidden below the surface of the ground. As a result, we have let an ancient skill-set languish from lack of use.

I'm here to tell you that you still have those skills to sense the hidden and unseen somewhere in your being, and I'm going to show you how to wake them up. Just stick with me through the following pages.

We call the skill-set used in finding underground water "dowsing," or more specifically "tangible dowsing," although our ancient ancestors would never have heard of such a term. In fact, we will use a variety of devices and aids that our ancestors would not have needed to use because the talented ones among them could just walk on the land and sense where to dig for water. The Indigenous People of Australia (among others) have maintained their ability to find hidden water sources in response to the arid nature of their lands.

The Bible tells the story of how God gave Moses instruction in dowsing to provide water for the Israelites:[1]:

> [2]Now there was no water for the congregation; so they gathered together against Moses and Aaron. [3]And the people contended with Moses and spoke, saying: "If only we had died when our brethren died before the Lord! [4]Why have you brought up the assembly of the Lord into this wilderness, that we and our animals should die here? [5]And why have you made us come up out of Egypt, to bring us to this evil place? It is not a place of grain or figs or vines or pomegranates; nor is there any water to drink." [6]So Moses and Aaron went from the presence of the assembly to the door of the tabernacle of meeting, and they fell on their faces. And the glory of the Lord appeared to them.
>
> [7]Then the Lord spoke to Moses, saying, [8]"Take the rod; you and your brother Aaron gather the congregation together. Speak to the rock before their eyes, and it will yield its water; thus you shall bring water for them out of the rock, and give drink to the congregation and their animals." [9]So Moses took the rod from before the Lord as He commanded him.

---

1   Numbers 20:2-11, King James Version.

> [10]And Moses and Aaron gathered the assembly together before the rock; and he said to them, "Hear now, you rebels! Must we bring water for you out of this rock?" [11]Then Moses lifted his hand and struck the rock twice with his rod; and water came out abundantly, and the congregation and their animals drank.

It is clear from the Bible passage above that dowsing is, indeed, an ancient skill that was practiced thousands of years ago. Also implicit in the story is that the ability to find drinkable water (in short, to be a dowser) was a requirement for a respected leader.

In our Western culture, which is under the sway of materialist science and technology, ancient skills like dowsing are considered to be flights of fancy. We are taught to believe only in the measurable input of our five physical senses. Since dowsing involves other senses, it has fallen into disrepute. Confronting this mistaken belief will be one of the greatest challenges we will face in this book.

Dowsing is an unknown territory for most modern humans, and no university courses have been developed so far. There are, however, many associations of dowsers in the UK and the USA. I'll list them in the Additional Resources (see p. 113). Many of these organizations offer training and opportunities to dowse with more experienced dowsers. For example, several UK dowsing groups meet on a regular basis to dowse in the countryside. It's a great way to get some hands-on experience with expert companions.

I have benefited greatly from studying with Dominic Susani (see p. 115) and Sig Lonegren (see p. 115), as well as dowsing in the field with a number of expert dowsers.

I need to say at the outset that this is not just another "how to" book about dowsing. I will teach you the mechanics of dowsing, but, beyond that, I am going to lead you deeply into your innermost being to awaken those expanded senses that you may have been taught that you do not have. I will be using terms like "the imaginal realm" and "the multi-dimensional realms" to describe the places you will visit using your expanded senses. You will be developing your Dowsing Mind, which will be the gateway to these realms. There is a logic to the progression we will follow, but it is the "organic" logic of the intuitive explorer, not the linear logic that appeals to the intellect.

The best way to use this book is to begin by reading through Part One, and then return and work through each section in detail. There will be experiments in dowsing on the land and anecdotes that will entertain and encourage contemplation. These experiments and anecdotes will alternate with sections of exposition about dowsing. I have structured this progression to enable you to enter and sustain the Dowsing Mind.

Parts Two, Three, and Four will lead you into more esoteric realms. You can use Part One alone or venture into the more exotic realms if you choose to do so. These more exotic sections will enhance your dowsing abilities, but they are not essential for dowsing in daily life.

I hope you are as excited about this exploration as I am. So, let's get started.

Part One

What Is Dowsing?

If you look in a dictionary, you will find that dowsing is defined as "a search for underground supplies of water, metal, etc., by the use of a divining rod." The definition usually goes on to talk about how dowsing is a pseudoscience that can't be confirmed by scientific means. I propose a new definition. Dowsing is "accessing the intuitive senses (Dowsing Mind) through the use of rods, pendulums, muscle testing, or direct sensation." It really doesn't make any difference if you use some device or your own body. The important thing is to gain access to your intuitive senses. Of course, intuitive senses are hard to confirm by nonintuitive, scientific means. If they weren't, they would not be intuitive! I will be calling your intuitive senses your "Dowsing Mind." And I will show you through numerous experiments that you do, indeed, have a Dowsing Mind and that it can be developed and educated.

Why Dowse?

There can be many reasons why you want to learn to dowse. You may simply be curious and want to try out this intriguing technique that you have heard about. Or you may have a need that you think dowsing might help you with, such as finding lost objects, selecting the most nutritious products to eat, helping to determine the source of physical or psychological symptoms, etc. Whatever your reason, welcome aboard a train that starts here in the "real" world and travels into realms that you may never have imagined existing. I will make the trip as interesting, fruitful, and fun as I can.

I will tell you at the outset, however, you will never become a dowser by reading this or any other book. Dowsing requires a lot of hands-on practice. For that reason, I will provide many experiments for you to try throughout this book.

Tangible and Intangible Dowsing

Tangible dowsing is looking for and locating objects or substances that are physical in nature. Examples are water, crude oil, minerals, lost objects, fault lines under the earth, and underground pipes. It is relatively easy to corroborate tangible dowsing when the object or substance is found in the location indicated by the dowser.

Intangible dowsing is dowsing for things that do not show themselves in easily recognizable physical form. Examples are earth energy lines, auras and energy centers around a person's body, information about products, and the like. This is a much murkier territory and does not lend itself to easy corroboration, although there are hi-tech instruments that can measure some of these intangibles. As we develop more and more sophisticated devices, many of the intangibles are becoming tangible.

It is important that you recognize that saying that something is "intangible" doesn't mean that it is just a flight of fancy and that it doesn't really exist. It's just that we can't easily corroborate it with our current measuring tools. We will explore both tangible and intangible dowsing in this book.

Dowsing Devices

Dowsing devices include the traditional Y-shaped willow or other tree branch, L-shaped rods or bent coat-hangers, and pendulums. All may be useful to you, but please understand that there is no magic in any of these tools or in the more expensive varieties that you can purchase at online dowsing supply sites. These are simply devices that amplify your intuitive responses and sometimes give you more specific information than you would have been able to access without them. They may help you to gain confidence in your developing skills. By using them and putting them away, you have a tangible reminder to return to the everyday world from "dowsing land." They can be a real assistance, so by all means use them. I still use my dowsing rods for much of the dowsing I do.

Traditional Forked Stick Dowsing Rod

The Dowsing Mind

One of the basic skills that our ancestors possessed and that we seldom use is intuition. My online dictionary defines intuition as "direct perception of truth, fact, etc., independent of any reasoning process; immediate apprehension." In other words, it is something you just "know" without thinking about it or thinking it through. In fact, as you will learn, intellectual processing will simply get in the way of your success as a dowser. I call the mental state that goes beyond your usual mental processing, your Dowsing Mind. People describe the Dowsing Mind as being naïvely curious, expecting the unexpected, blank, free from thought, unattached to outcome, still, and many other terms. Developing your Dowsing Mind is the primary objective of this book. I am still developing my Dowsing Mind after many years of dowsing.

Left Brain vs Right Brain

In the 20th century, neuro-scientists who were seeking to understand how our brains work developed the theory that the left brain was used for intellectual work, such as reading, counting, data processing, and speaking, while the right brain was used for artistic pursuits, emotional tasks, and feelings. Later research has shown that this division was simplistic, and our brains are much more complex than these scientists thought. Recently, the simplistic dichotomy has been updated by the eminent Scottish psychiatrist/philosopher Iain McGilchrist. Author Gary Lachman says:

> "Put briefly, our right brain, which McGilchrist contends is older and primary—it is the 'master'of his title—sees the world as a whole, as a given totality, a living presence, much as we see another person. In Pascal's terms, it sees things intuitively, 'at a glance.' It is interested in implicit meanings. Because of this, its picture is somewhat 'fuzzy.' It has a general, indubitable sense of 'meaning,' yet it cannot articulate it in any detail—much like the implicit meanings in music that we cannot articulate explicitly. That is the job of the left brain, McGilchrist's 'emissary'" (Lachman, *Lost Knowledge of the Imagination,* 2017, p. 17).

It is this left- and right-brain distinction I am using in this book.

To be successful at dowsing you need to be able to "turn off" your left (verbal) brain and allow your right (intuitive) brain free reign. Given the way most of us have been trained to emphasize left-brain processes, this is not easily accomplished.

When you begin to dowse, you are likely to try to "figure out" the correct answer using your left brain. That will always fail. Instead, you must make your mind blank and act as if you are neutral about the outcome. That state of neutrality is where you will find the Dowsing Mind.

Neural Oscillations

Another way of talking about different states of mind is the well-known phenomenon of neural oscillations. Our brains produce tiny, but measurable, electrical charges that vibrate at different frequencies. Several bands of frequencies have been identified, including the delta (1-4 Hz), the theta (4-8 Hz), the alpha (8-12 Hz), the beta (13-30 Hz), and the gamma (30-150 Hz). Our normal waking state usually produces frequencies in the alpha band, while dowsing and meditation produces frequencies in the theta band. Your Dowsing Mind is in the theta band of frequencies.

Harmonizing with Your Surroundings

To be successful at dowsing you must learn to become "at one" with the environment around you. Animals are masters of this. They use techniques to hide from their enemies and approach their prey without being noticed. Octopuses change color at will and even display complex patterns all over their bodies to match their backgrounds and become nearly invisible. The chameleon lizard is so adept at this skill that we often call a person a "chameleon" who changes their personality to match the people they are with. You won't need to be able to change your spots to be a successful dowser, but the internal process is much like that. I will have much more to say about this when we deal with resonance in later sections.

Asking Permission

Before beginning any dowsing practice, it is important to ask permission to do so. At this point I will leave open the issue of who or what to seek permission from, although I will have more to say about that later. For now, simply ask yourself, "Am I ready to do this work?" Wait for an inner feeling of "yes" before proceeding. Asking permission puts you in the proper mental state to enter the Dowsing Mind.

Experiment #1: Pausing the Left Brain

Equipment needed: a clock or watch that registers every second. It can have a sweep second hand or a digital counter.

Goal: to extend the time your mind is blank.

The assignment is to notice every thought that comes into your head. If you pay attention, you can notice every thought as it happens. Look at the watch or clock and take note of each thought that your left brain generates. Try to maximize the time between thoughts. Is it two seconds? Can you raise it to five seconds? Get a feel for what those "blank" periods—the space between thoughts—are like. Feel into those blanks. That is what dowsing feels like. If you have trouble staying blank, try staring at a white wall that has nothing on it to distract you. You can learn to stay blank for longer and longer times, but it takes practice. Try thinking "blank, blank, blank, blank, . . ." for a minute.

Become inventive. Create a way to make your mind blank. You have to trick your left brain into pausing the ongoing stream of thoughts. Sometimes concentrating on your breath will do it. Or imagine fog so thick that you can't see anything, or clouds floating by in a blue sky. Just let those clouds roll by. Make a game out of stopping your left brain. Have fun!

Why Do We Need to Pause the Left Brain?

It is in the blank (still) area between thoughts that you will discover the Dowsing Mind. It is there, just waiting to be activated, so go for it! Or, in terms of brain waves, it is entering the theta state.

Another way of saying the same thing (or nearly the same thing, if you want to be persnickety about it) is to call the ongoing stream of thoughts "living in the 3-D world," while entering the Dowsing Mind is learning to sense into the "multi-dimensional" world. I sometimes say I "go multi-dimensional," although I am not traveling anywhere physically. As you can see already, this stuff is really difficult to talk about. Relax. Don't get caught up in the language. Have fun.

I use the term "3-D world" to indicate the everyday reality that we live in. It is the world of three dimensions: length, breadth, and depth. This is where you are right now.

What Are These Multi-Dimensional Realms?

The second part of this book will deal extensively with the multi-dimensional realms, but I will give a brief introduction at this point. The multi-dimensional realms are places our consciousness can go that are outside the 3-D limitations of our physical bodies. They are realms well-traversed by Christian mystics, Sufi philosophers, shamans, and Western mystery school adepts. The master dream explorer Robert Moss says, "If we call something 'imaginary,' we usually mean it is 'made up,' something other than 'real.' Yet poets and mystics have always known that the world of imagination is a real world—a third kingdom between the physical universe and the higher realms of spirit—and that it is possible to travel there and bring back extraordinary gifts" (Moss, *Dreamgates*, 1998, pp. 115-116). That is what I am calling the multi-dimensional realms. Christian theologian Rev. Dr. Cynthia Bourgeault says, "... The imaginal is always understood within traditional metaphysics to be objectively real ... a sphere that is not less real but more real than our so-called 'objective reality' ..." (Northwestwisdom.org/2015/12/is-the-imaginal-realm-real/).

Two short examples will illustrate what I am talking about. Every night when you go to sleep, your consciousness leaves your physical body lying on the bed while you enter dreamland. In that space/place, you travel and have adventures and encounters that are a mix of elements taken from your waking experience and elements that are unlike anything you have seen before. You enter multi-dimensional realms in your dreams.

People who have near-death experiences commonly report that they were outside their bodies and looking on as their doctors struggled to bring them back to this world. When they are outside looking down on their bodies, I would say that they are viewing from a multi-dimensional perspective.

Experiment #2: Stillness Meditation

Equipment needed: a still mind.

Goal: further development of the Dowsing Mind.

You may find this stillness meditation, which is reprinted here with the permission of R. J. Stewart,[2] useful in stopping the left brain. In the spaces between thoughts, you may be able to sense the Dowsing Mind. It can feel like something that is going on in your consciousness while the mind is resting. Try remaining blank for as long as possible during and after this meditation.

(You may find it helpful to record this practice and play it back as you do the practice.)

---

2   https://rjstewart.org/inner-temples-meditations/

1. Breathing steadily, align yourself to the directions: above, below. Then: Before you, behind you, to your right, to your left, and the center within.

2. Still your sense of time, of space, and of movement. Breathe steadily, letting go of time, space, and movement.

3. Reach into the stillness within, beyond all time, space, and movement.

4. Chant the vowel sounds O, A, I, three times, elongating the vowels on one steady tone. (The "O" stills time. The "A" draws in space to the center. The "I" stills all movement.)

5. Be still, reach into the Void of Un-Being, out of which all being comes. (Rest here in stillness for 5-10 minutes.)

6. Affirm again the directions (as in #1).

7. Close your meditation and return to the outer world. Or proceed with your intended spiritual/magical/meditational working, bringing it to life out of the Stillness.

You will be developing your Dowsing Mind as you work through the following experiments. The experiments I'm suggesting have been very helpful to me in developing my skills as a dowser, but they may or may not work for you.

Experiment #3: Practicing with a Pendulum

Equipment needed: a pendulum.

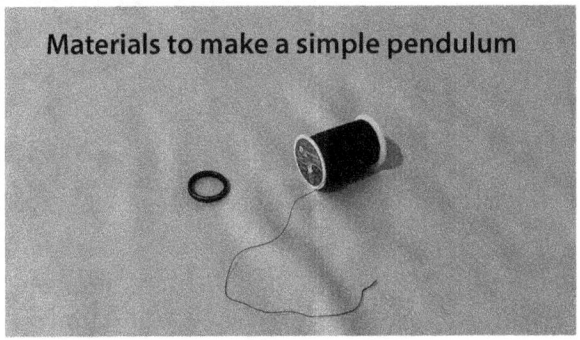

Materials to make a simple pendulum

Goal: to develop the feel for pendulum dowsing.

Now we´ll get down to the nitty gritty of dowsing with an exercise to give you a feel for what I´m talking about. Let´s start by dowsing with a pendulum. Get out your pendulum or make one. It doesn´t have to be anything fancy. If you don´t own a pendulum, you can make one by tying a thread, a strand of hair, or a light-weight string to a ring or other small object. You will need about six or seven inches of thread or string to hold onto so that the pendulum can swing freely. (We will talk in greater detail about various types of pendulums later in the book.)

Hold your pendulum in your dominant hand (left or right, depending on which hand you use for writing), or use whichever hand works better for you. Let the string or thread hang down between your thumb and first and/or second fingers, the fingers in a slightly downward position. It is important that you be comfortable with this position, so experiment until it feels right. Think of your pendulum as an extension of your body. It will be connected with your Dowsing Mind and will report on what is going on in your Dowsing Mind.

Pendulum in search position

Hold the pendulum steady until it stops swinging. We call this your "search position." This is the position you want the pendulum in before you ask any question.

Now enter your Dowsing Mind (remember—go into that inner place of stillness that you practiced in Experiments 1 and 2) and ask the pendulum, "Show me your 'yes.'" Observe how the pendulum responds. It may begin to circle in a clockwise or counterclockwise direction, or it may begin to swing from side to side or back and forth. Don't think about it. Just let the pendulum do its thing. Make note of the pendulum's "yes" movement.

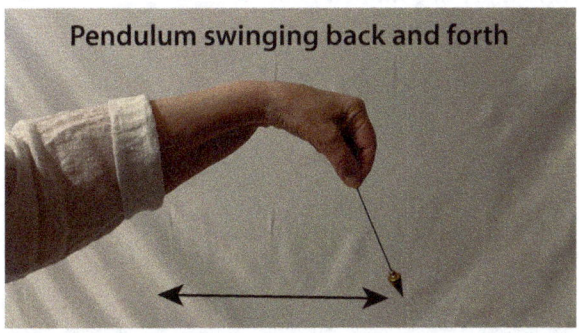

Pendulum swinging back and forth

Now let the pendulum stop moving (return to search position), go into your Dowsing Mind, and ask, "Show me your 'no.'" Observe how the pendulum responds. It may move in any of the above directions. If it is the same as the "yes" direction, you will need to start the process again because you have gotten a contradictory response. Remember: your "yes" and "no" movements are yours alone. They may not be the same as another dowser's movements.

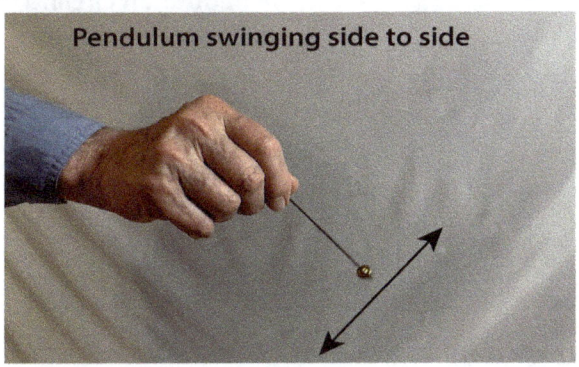

Pendulum swinging side to side

Once you are clear about the "yes" and "no" movements of your pendulum, you can ask a series of questions or make a series of statements. For example:

"My name is (your name)."

"My name is (a fictious name)."

"It´s raining outside my window."

"I have a pet dog named Pooch."

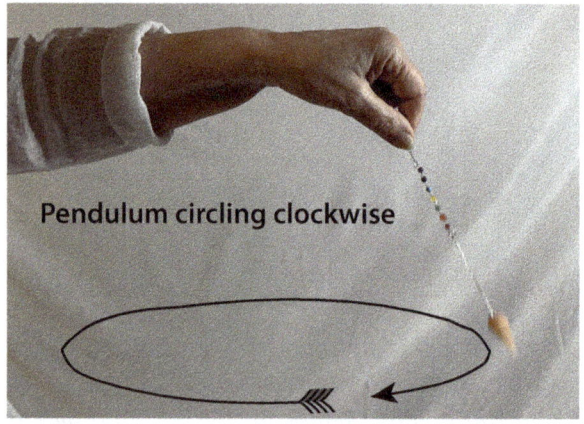

After each statement, wait for the pendulum to respond. Does it give you the correct "yes" and "no" answers to these statements? If not, try again, making sure that you go to your Dowsing Mind each time.

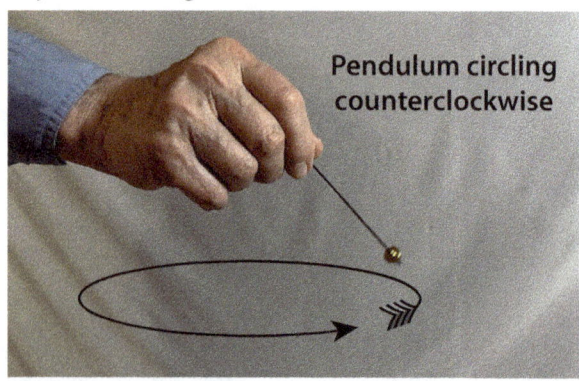

"My age is (your age)."

"My age is (a false age)."

"My hair is red."

"I live in New York City."

"I drive a Toyota car."

"I am an elementary school teacher."

Make up other "yes" or "no" questions or statements, and observe the answers provided by the pendulum. Keep practicing until you get correct answers, making sure you go to your Dowsing Mind each time you ask.

But I Can Make the Pendulum Do Anything I Want It To!

Of course you can! All you have to do is hold the pendulum and tell it to spin clockwise and, sure enough, in a few seconds it will begin to turn as your finger muscles subtly twitch to respond to your command. Anyone can do that, but that is simply connecting your left brain to the pendulum. That's not dowsing, that's trickery! What you must do if you want to use the pendulum to dowse is "turn off" your left brain (hit the virtual "pause" button) and connect to the pendulum with your Dowsing Mind. Let your Dowsing Mind do the talking, and you will be dowsing in no time. I'm going to be saying this in a hundred different ways until you get it.

What Is Going on Here?

Your Dowsing Mind knows the correct answer to each of the questions you are asking, and the Dowsing Mind will subtly influence the response of the pendulum. In other words, the pendulum is just a tool to report "from" your Dowsing Mind. The pendulum lets you see what the Dowsing Mind knows. The pendulum "amplifies" your interior knowledge, which is transmitted as nerve signals to your muscles, which respond and influence the motion of the pendulum.

When you get good at this, you can use the pendulum to answer questions that your conscious mind doesn't know the answers to but your Dowsing Mind does. It will seem that the pendulum moves on its own. This isn't magic, it's dowsing! And when you get really good at it, you can stop using the pendulum and just consult your Dowsing Mind. Then you can use the dowsing tool or not, depending on your preference at the moment.

Experiment #4: L-shaped Rods

Equipment needed: a pair of L-shaped dowsing rods.

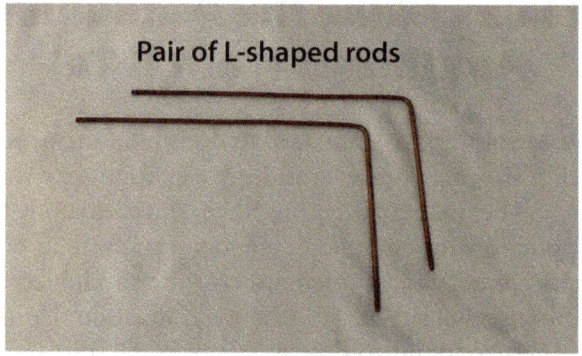

Goal: to get used to using the L-shaped rods.

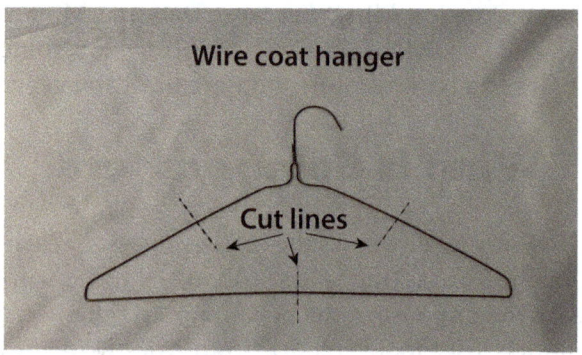

For this next exercise you're going to need a pair of L-shaped rods. If you don't own a pair, go to your clothes closet and choose a wire shirt or blouse hanger. You're going to need one that is entirely metal—no plastic or paper for this one. Get out a pair of wire cutters and cut

the coat hanger as shown in the illustration. Discard the extra piece and bend the two remaining sections into a pair of L-shaped rods. Trim the handles to a comfortable length for your hands. These are your tools for this exercice.

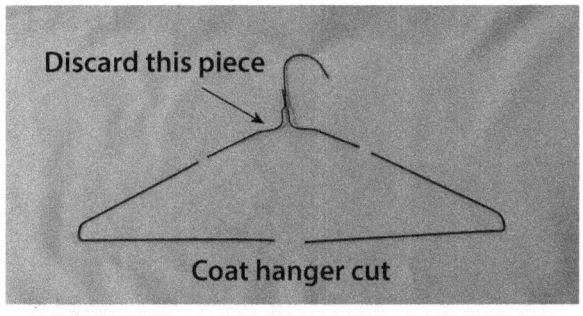

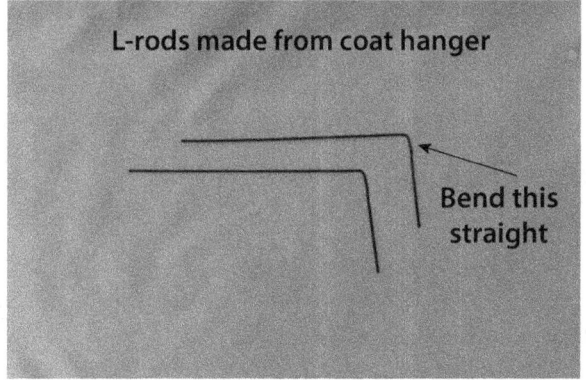

The first thing you need to learn is how to hold the rods. Hold one rod in each hand with the longer ends of the L facing away from you. Allow enough space between them so the rods won't get in each other's way. Find a comfortable position with your elbows at your sides. It is important that you grasp the rods tight enough so that they won't slip away from you, while still allowing them to swing freely. If you grasp them too tightly, they won't move at all. If you hold them too loosely, you will end up dropping them. Some store-bought rods have a built-in sleeve over the handle that allows you to grip them as *tightly as you want while still leaving the L's free to move about.*

Next, you need to find the "sweet spot" of your rods. If you raise the tips up slightly, the rods will swing open or closed. "Open" means they swing in opposite directions, away from each other, and "closed" means they swing toward each other and cross. Or they may swing in the same direction. None of these three movements is a good position for dowsing since the motion of the rods is simply their response to gravity.

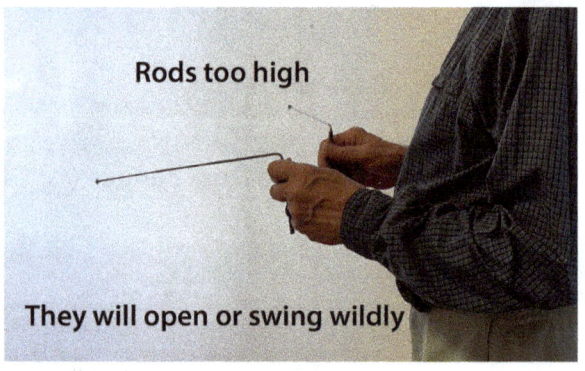

If, on the other hand, you lower the tips of the rods an inch or two, so they point downward, the rods won't swing at all because they would have to move upward against gravity. That also is not a good dowsing position. The "sweet spot" is just between those two positions and almost parallel with the ground. It is where the rods can swing freely but don't swing wildly in either direction. You need to find that sweet spot because it is the correct position for dowsing with rods. It will be unique for every set of rods and every way you grip them, so just experiment until your find the sweet spot for the rods in your hands. We will call this sweet spot with the L's pointing straight ahead, the "search" position.

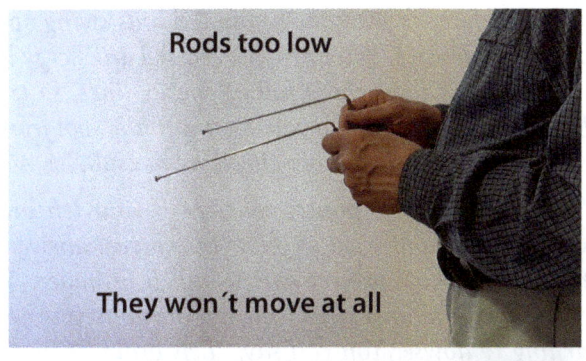

Rods too low

They won´t move at all

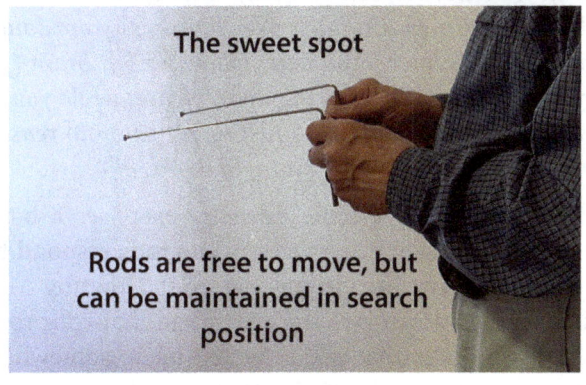

The sweet spot

Rods are free to move, but can be maintained in search position

Now for your first exercise. Go to some place where you have room to walk. Your local public park is ideal, if you don´t mind people´s curious stares. Otherwise, just choose the largest open space in your apartment or house. Take your L-rods in your hands and find their sweet spot. Mentally ask the rods to show you an energy line in the earth under your house, apartment, or the space you are in. For now, don´t worry about what kind of energy line it might be, or even what an energy line is.

Now ask permission, and think (or say aloud) the following statement: "Rods, show me an energy line here in my apartment (or wherever you happen to be)." (Get used to talking to inanimate objects. You will be doing a lot of that later in this book!) Go to your Dowsing Mind, and begin walking forward with rods in hand. You prob-

ably won't have to walk far before the rods swing open, closed, or sideways. You have just crossed an energy line of some sort. The world is full of energy lines, so trust what the rods just showed you. Come at the spot from a different direction to double-check your result.

If you don't get a response, consider if your left brain got in the way and tried to guess the correct answer or decided the whole project was a bunch of hooey. You need to be quite firm with your left brain as you begin learning to dowse. You can say, "Left brain, your only job here is to remain quiet. We'll address your doubts and questions later." You can "tell" your left brain (figuratively) to wait outside the door, please, while you do this work. If your left brain just won't listen to reason, you can always say, "Left brain, SHUT UP!"

We'll get into more specific dowsing exercises a bit later, but for now just have fun watching the rods respond to the Earth's energy. Try imagining that your Dowsing Mind is sending a signal down into the Earth and that your rods are reading the signals that are reflected back, somewhat like ground penetrating radar (GPR) that is used to detect underground objects. That should help you get a feel for dowsing.

It is important that you get used to the feel of the rods seeming to move on their own. There is nothing supernatural or spooky about this. I'll give you a perfectly reasonable explanation a bit later. For now, just do this exercise over and over, and curb your curious left brain that wants to know what is really going on and what sort of energy lines you might be crossing.

I urge you to stop reading the book at this point and practice. Don't forget to still your left brain and go to your Dowsing Mind every time you dowse. Believe me, it will help you greatly when you are learning to do more challenging things in the later sections of this book.

You can work with your rods in a similar way as you did with the pendulum. You can establish your rods' "yes" and "no" and go through all the same statements and questions you did before (see p. 16). The rods will work in nearly the same way as the pendulum. However, I find that I need to be standing and walking for good results with rods, whereas I can work with a pendulum while standing still or even when seated. You may find it interesting to explore which device gives you the best results. These matters are quite personal. In most of the remaining exercises in the book I'll assume you are working with rods, but if you prefer the pendulum, you can use it for the exercises just as well.

Remember:

- Ask permission: "Am I ready to do this?"
- Rods in search position.
- State what you're looking for. For example, "Show me an energy line."
- Go to your Dowsing Mind.
- Walk forward until the rods give you a "yes."
- Check your results by crossing that point again from a different direction.

Dowsing with a Purpose

I feel sure that our ancestors first discovered the skill that we now call dowsing in their search for water. Water is second only to air as essential for life. But after they had finding water down pat, they must have also used the skill to search for other things they needed or wanted, like food or animals. They probably used dowsing to locate pigments (like ochre) to make their art, stones that could be made into tools, and a thousand other items to enhance their lifestyle. "Ask and it shall be given you. Seek, and ye shall find. Knock, and it shall be opened unto you."[3] In our other words: "Dowse and you will find what you seek."

---

3 Matthew 7:7, King James Version.

Dowsing for Information

Dowsers use their skills in a variety of ways, including dowsing for information, which is intangible dowsing. They ask "yes" and "no" questions such as, "Is this vitamin supplement the very best for me today?" Or, "Is this the best set of hiking shoes for me to buy for walking the trails near my home?" Always ask the simplest and clearest "yes" or "no" questions you can construct, and you will get the best answers. Like a binary computer, dowsing can only answer "yes" or "no" to a single question. The following list contains other examples that can stimulate you to create your own questions.

- "Is it in my highest interest to move away from this neighborhood now?" (You can see that if you leave off "now," your answer will be incomplete.)
- "Is it in my highest interest to start the search for a different job this year?"
- "Out of all the melons in this store, is this the tastiest melon for me to buy?"
- "Is this the best price I can find for this new computer?"

Practice dowsing for information to gain confidence in your skills.

There are many dowsing techniques. Some are not obvious to people around you, so you can even dowse while shopping at your local grocery store or on a visit to a sacred site. I'll mention a few of these other techniques later in the book (see pp. 53-54).

Visualization

Visualization is the act of creating a clear mental image of what you want to find or do. Athletes visualize their perfect performance, and it has been scientifically proven that their performance improves remarkably as a result. Form a clear mental image of what you are dowsing for, and the rods will guide you to it.

Let's say you are seeking underground water. You will mentally give your rods an order that when you walk over underground water, they are to move in a particular way. For instance, "When I walk over water, swing open." A clear mental image of what that underground water might look like will help the process, so visualize an underground stream of water. Of course, underground water comes in many forms, from flowing creeks and rivers resembling surface water features, to still pools similar to the ponds and lakes on the Earth's surface. Underground pipes carry water to and from buildings. It probably won't make much difference in the process of visualization, but a large underground body of water can be quite confusing to dowse because you may not be able to sense a beginning and an end to it. You can choose a very specific form of underground water, or keep it more general and dowse for water in any form.

I employ a variety of physical adjuncts to visualization when I'm looking for water. For example, I sometimes hold the rods low in front of my abdomen in the area of my kidneys and bladder as a physiological reminder of what I'm looking for. I may stimulate production of saliva in my mouth as another nonverbal reminder. One dowser I know senses underground water in the back of his knees. The advantage of these techniques is that they are physiological and nonverbal, which helps keep the analytical left brain out of the picture. You can invent your own techniques and find which will work best for you. There are no hard-and-fast rules to this game. The only goal is success in finding what you are seeking.

I can guess that your left brain will react just like mine did when I first learned to dowse. We are so used to "figuring things out" that our left brain springs into action at every opportunity. You need to be quite firm with your left brain and tell it that its job at this time is to get out of the way. Tell it,

"You won't be able to figure this one out, so just stop trying." Leave your skepticism at the door. You can always come back for it later!

Experiment #5: Another L-rod Exercise

Equipment needed: a pair of L-rods.

Goal: to practice dowsing for water.

You will need to find some area outdoors where you can walk over considerable land to practice water dowsing. If you are shy about showing yourself outdoors with dowsing rods in your hands, you'll have to get creative about choosing a time and place with few if any people about.

If you don't know of an outdoor place to practice dowsing for water, you can be successful indoors if you know where the water pipes are located under the floor of your apartment or house. Water is water, whether it lies beneath the surface of the Earth or is running through a metal pipe in your apartment. You can consult city maps or a blueprint of your house to find out where accessible water lines are located.

When you have chosen an area or location and asked permission, say this to your rods: "When my foot (or the tips of my rods) reaches the edge of a water source, swing open." Hold the rods in search position and find their sweet spot. Go to your Dowsing Mind (don't forget to activate your imaginary ground penetrating radar) and start walking. Take note of where you are when the rods swing open. Trust what the rods tell you, but walk across that same place from a different angle just to check the result. You may be able to sense the two edges if you keep walking after the rods have moved. They may snap back to search position at the other edge of the stream. And yes, you can ask your rods to show you the depth or the direction of flow, but that comes later. You have just completed your first experience of dowsing for water. Congratulations!

Getting It Set in Your System

Now you just need to practice until the process becomes "set" in your system. Learning to dowse is a little like learning to ride a bicycle. At first, it requires your full attention; but as it becomes familiar, you will do all the preparations automatically, without thinking about it. It will take several practice sessions over a few weeks or more to do so, so don't try to hurry the process by going on to the next exercise. Let this one settle in. It is a big one.

When you can get yourself ready to dowse more or less automatically, you will know that you can go on to the next steps. Besides, you can have fun and enjoy the process of learning, so why hurry?

Here is a summary of the process of dowsing as I have presented it so far.

Remember:

- Ask permission: "Am I ready to do this?"
- Rods in search position.
- State what you are looking for: "Show me a source of water."
- Enter your Dowsing Mind (and activate your imaginary GPR).
- Walk forward until the rods give you a "yes."
- Check your result by crossing that point again from a different direction.

Remember that you are shifting between the everyday, 3-D world and the multi-dimensional realm each time you enter your Dowsing Mind. You will feel a sensed shift each time you do this, and it takes time to get used to making the shift. In terms of your brainwaves, it is a shift from your normal (alpha) waking state to the Dowsing Mind in the theta realm. This is a major shift and, at first, it requires conscious attention.

I often find taking a conscious deep breath helpful as I make the shift into and out of the Dowsing Mind. Breath is much more than simply the way we take in oxygen and release carbon dioxide. It is fundamental to living and can be a way to shift your consciousness. Try taking a conscious deep breath, holding it, and then releasing it. Do you see how your consciousness shifts?

Practical Dowsing

If you are thinking that this dowsing business is all just "woogie woogie," consider that oil companies pay dowsers good money to locate places to "wildcat" drill for oil. Oil companies are not known for their generosity, so they must feel they get their money's worth when they hire dowsers.

I know a person who was trying to sell a piece of land in a very rural area of northern New Mexico. There was no apparent water on the property, and he realized that he could get a much better price if he could drill a well that would be a good water source. He hired a local dowser to locate the water and received a report showing the exact location to drill and the depth where the water would be found. He contracted a driller, who found water precisely where the dowser said it would be. He sold the property at a nice profit.

What's Really Going on

While you are getting the "feel" of dowsing imbedded in your system, it is good time to give your left brain a little treat and discuss what is really going on when you dowse for water. Far from what it may appear to be, dowsing is not some magical act. As a human being, you have hidden somewhere in your subconscious mind your ancestors' skills at finding drinking water. This skill has never been activated because you probably have a ready supply of more or less drinkable water in the kitchen—maybe even on your refrigerator door. When you are dowsing, your Dowsing Mind is sending the information it knows about the location of underground water to your hands in the form of subtle nerve impulses. These signals are amplified by the dowsing tool in your hands.

Your body may be unconsciously sensing very subtle shifts in the electromagnetic field, shifts in humidity levels, or other subtle cues that provide information about the location of underground water. I know you would like to know exactly how this process works. So would I, but, in spite of the fact that I don't know how it works, I have come to trust that it does work, even though I can't explain it. If your conscious, logic-seeking (left brain) mind is switched off, your hands can respond to those subtle signals and move the rods according to the instructions your Dowsing Mind has given them. The rods will swing open or closed, depending on how you have programmed them. Notice the reference to computer programming. That is a good way to think about how you ask your rods to respond. You program them with your left brain, then hit pause, and allow the Dowsing Mind to do the work.

The fact that your hands react is not cheating. It is just letting a part of your sensory system that hasn't been activated before swing into action. You have to get the left brain out of the way to let this happen. It takes considerable practice to get this new way of using your nervous system set in your body. When you really get this new way of sensing perfected, you may even be able to allow your left brain to think a little while you are dowsing, but you must keep a strong rein on it or it will run wild and shut the whole process down.

There, doesn't that feel better? Your left brain has something to chew on, and it may even let you continue to practice this new (and at the same time, very old) set of skills. When you get really good at this, you may even be able to leave the rods at home and sense underground water just like our ancestors did 20,000 years ago. Personally, I still prefer having the rods in my hands when I dowse. But I only take out the rods after

I've spent some time walking the land and "sensing" what is there with my Dowsing Mind.

I have an amusing story to share with you about my dowsing rods.

Faery Magic

I usually keep my portable set of dowsing rods in my jacket pocket when I'm out walking the land. One day when I reached in to get them, they weren't there. I checked every pocket in vain. What to do? Well, I thought, maybe I should see if I could do some dowsing without them. I began using my open hands to sense what I wanted to dowse for and, sure enough, I could feel the energies fairly well as very subtle pressure on the palms of my hands. About 15 minutes later, I put my hands in my pocket, and the dowsing rods were back in their usual place! I think that the faeries were playing a little trick on me by taking my rods away, just so I could prove to myself that I could work without them. Thanks, guys, you gave me a valuable lesson, and we all had some fun.

That is not the only time the faeries have taken away my rods. I was recently walking the land in northern Arizona with my wife, Elyn, and a friend. I had been demonstrating dowsing and teaching our friend a bit about it. I put the rod I was using in a jacket pocket, and a few minutes later reached for it. The faeries had taken it again. The rod returned about 15 minutes later, where it had been before. I don't know exactly what the message was, but it certainly has something to do with reminding me how optional the rods really are. They enhance and amplify what the body senses, and they make it easier to get additional, more precise information (depth of water and direction of flow, for example), but that is all.

Dowsing for Lines

So far, we have been concentrating solely on dowsing for water. Now we will add other search-topics to the mix. You might ask, "How can one set of rods distinguish among such diverse phenomena as water, fault lines, energy grids, and all the other things I might want to dowse for?" The secret lies in your intention. In other words, it's not the rods but *you* who decides what to look for.

Intention

Wikipedia defines intention as "a mental state that represents a commitment to carrying out an action or actions in the future." I like this definition because it contains two words that I will have several things to say about: "mental" and "future." First, mental. "Mental," in our terms, means left brain (finally, some real work for the left brain to do). To create an intention, we fire up the good old left brain and state an intention: "I want to dowse for . . . ." Now, for the "future" part. You shut the left brain down and go to your Dowsing Mind. In the Dowsing Mind you do your usual preparation for dowsing. This is "in the future" because you paused the left brain and went through the preparation process, and that took some time. This clearly separates the act of dowsing from the act of thinking about what you are wanting to dowse for. As you know so well by now, you can't be dowsing and thinking at the same time—at least not yet.

Notice the mental gymnastics we are going through in dowsing. We usually just let our mental processes proceed however they will, without our conscious intervention. Dowsing is all about intentionally shifting our consciousness from analytic thinking to the Dowsing Mind. As you practice, you will get better and better at this process of shifting into the Dowsing Mind and back to the left brain. It may even become fun and something you will want to do for other purposes, like meditation, for instance. Remember that you can use conscious breathing to aid you in making the shifts. Try breathing in slowly, holding for a moment, and breathing out slowly. Notice how the mind stops while you are holding the breath. 5-10 minutes of this breathing practice will certainly shift your consciousness.

Experiment #6: Dowsing for a Piece of Yarn

Equipment needed: dowsing rods and a piece of yarn or string, some rugs or newspapers.

Goal: more practice for field dowsing.

This experiment, which you can do at home, will give you more practice for dowsing in the field. Take a piece of yarn about 3 feet in length. It can be any old piece of yarn or string you have around the house. Stretch it out on the floor and cover it with a throw rug or a few newspapers. Take your dowsing rods and go through your preparation: ask permission, put your rods in search position, and state your intention: "When my foot (or the tips of my rods) comes to the piece of yarn (or string), I want the rods to open up (or close)." Now, go to your Dowsing Mind and walk over the rug or newspapers. Did the rods respond? Try it again. Success? Try it with something else.

Get a friend to set up the exercise for you so you won't know exactly where the object is. Maybe they can put down multiple newspapers so you won't know which one covers the piece of yarn. You can make up other variations on this experiment. Keep working at it until you get consistent, positive results. As they say, practice makes perfect, whether you are learning to ride a bike or learning to dowse. You are building your "dowsing muscles," so practice regularly.

Remember:

- Ask permission: "Am I ready to do this?"
- Rods in search position.

- State your intention: "Show me the piece of yarn."
- Go to your Dowsing Mind (remember your "ground penetrating radar").
- Walk forward until the rods give you a "yes."
- Check your result by crossing that point again from a different direction.

Grounding Techniques

When you come back from your Dowsing Mind, you are likely to be a bit dizzy or disoriented. For this reason, it is important to ground yourself back in the 3-D world. There are many techniques for grounding yourself, but here are a few that I have used. A traditional technique that I have found to be effective is to stare at my feet while standing on the ground. I take a few deep breaths and then look up at the 3-D world around me. That often brings me back. Or simply take in three or four deep breaths and release them. You can rub your arms and legs briskly, or stretch your arms, legs, and toes to become aware of your body.

When I prepare to drive a car or operate any equipment after dowsing, I always ground myself and check to make sure I am back in everyday reality.

Fault Lines

Much of the surface of the Earth is covered with a subterranean layer of bedrock. If you dig down, sooner or later you will come to solid rock. When you drive on a highway, you will sometimes see the bedrock showing through in the cuts that have been made in the Earth to make the highway more or less level. That sedimentary rock was once a continuous layer, but over the millions of years since its deposit, usually at the bottom of an ancient sea, the Earth has continued to heave and move, which likely caused cracks to form in the bedrock. Geologists call these cracks "faults."

Over the millennia, there may have been movement along these cracks, and the layers may have shifted up or down relative to each other, or they may have slipped sideways. Geologists are very interested in these shifts. We are going to learn how to sense these faults. It won't make any difference to us right now what caused them and how they have moved.

Some faults are huge, and when they slip and slide, they cause earthquakes. In the USA, for example, the largest fault is the San Andreas Fault in California. That fault was responsible for the devastating earthquakes that hit San Francisco in 1906 and again in 1989. Other faults are much smaller, and some are scarcely noticeable cracks in the bedrock. We don't care whether the faults we are going to sense are as big as the San Andreas or just a tiny crack a few yards long. In fact, if you were to dowse the San Andreas fault you might find it is several yards wide in places. Large or small, they are all faults. Sometimes you can actually see faults on the surface, for example, in Iceland in the Continental Rift Valley, which is 230 feet wide, but most are hidden from view.

Experiment #7: Fault Lines

Equipment needed: dowsing rods.

Goal: finding a fault line.

Take your rods and find a good spot outdoors where you can walk for a distance. The place you chose before (if you did) will work just fine. Ask permission, put the rods in search position, state your intention: "When my foot reaches a fault, I want the rods to open up." Now go to your Dowsing Mind, set your GPR to look for faults, and begin to walk slowly and steadily.

Take note of any movement in the rods. If they respond as you programmed them to, you may have crossed a fault line. Try dowsing from a different angle and see if the rods act the same way. If so, you have found a fault line. Congratulations! If not, you may have been mistaken on one of your passes. If you are unsure, try a third time and take the response that agrees with one of your previous tries as correct.

Remember:

- Ask permission: "Am I ready to do this?"
- Rods in search position.
- State your intention: "When my foot is over a fault I want the rods to open up."
- Go to your Dowsing Mind (and remember your GPR).
- Walk forward until the rods give you a "yes."
- Check your result by crossing that point again from a different direction.

You can do the same exercise with a pendulum. Just program the above indicators appropriately. For example, crossing a fault line might be indicated by a shift in the pendulum from its search position to its "yes" movement, or from "no" to "yes."

Experiment #8: Discovering the Orientation of a Fault

You might want to explore the orientation of the fault. To do so, tell your rods to follow the fault. Return them to search position, and turn so that the rods are pointing in the direction you believe the fault goes. As you walk along, notice any shifting of the rods to the left or right. Follow the direction they point, and you are following the fault line. It is possible that you will walk to the end of the fault if it is a small one. In my experience, the rods will open at that point, but you will have to see what happens for you. Check around the area to see if you can find the fault again or if the fault has, indeed, terminated.

If you have been dowsing with a pendulum, you will need to devise some other method of following the fault line. For example, you might swing the pendulum in the direction you think the fault is going and watch when it begins to veer to the left or right. Be creative. You can find your own way to be successful.

If you have dowsed this area for water before, you may find that the fault line is in the same location as the water line. Water often runs through these cracks in the bedrock, and we call these faults "wet faults." If the fault you just found is at a location where you didn't find water, we call it a "dry fault." Another word for a dry fault line that some dowsers use is "fire line." Why they use that term is unclear to me, but I've heard it used by more than one dowser, and I sometimes use it myself. Perhaps it comes from a recognition that faults are often caused by molten lava intruding into bedrock. Some dowsers recognize a category of faults they call "damp faults." They often say that "damp faults" are unhealthy and should be avoided.

In truth, the names various dowsers give to the faults they encounter vary widely. It depends on who the dowser studied with and what their teacher called the faults. When I have dowsed with other experienced dowsers, we can generally come to some agreement about the nature of particular faults. For example, I dowsed with a person who identified all faults as either masculine or feminine. I would call his masculine faults dry faults or fire lines, and his feminine faults wet faults. We discovered that we were usually in agreement even though we used different terms.

Dowsing for More

Now that you have learned to bring your intention to your dowsing, you can try dowsing for different things. Just set your intention and go for it! You might try to locate the roots of a tree that has died and left nothing on the surface. Or you might try to locate metal objects in the ground. Can you locate buried pieces of glass? You can have fun and enjoy the adventure. It is all good practice, and the more you do it, the more dowsing will become second nature to you.

The skill you are developing is, in part, the skill of shifting your consciousness from its normal left-brain mode to the Dowsing Mind. At the same time, you are also becoming more and more familiar with the feel of the rods (or pendulum) in your hands. Soon you will automatically go through the preparation process without even thinking about it, like the way you drive your car or ride a bike.

Remember:

- Ask permission: "Am I ready to do this?"
- Rods in search position.
- State your intention: "Show me . . . ."
- Go to your Dowsing Mind.
- Walk forward until the rods give you a "yes."

Each of us comes to dowsing with a unique set of skills. Mine, for example, comes from my extensive training as a musician and composer. As a musician, I was trained to be extremely sensitive to sound. I was required to play and sing exactly in tune and in time with the musicians around me, and to make my sound blend with the ensemble so that my contribution to the sound that listeners heard was unnoticeable. Only when I was the soloist could I allow my sound to predominate, and I learned techniques for standing out from the crowd. Being a performing musician requires unrelenting attention to details of sound. As a result, I am usually aware of my sound environment in ways that escape the attention of most other people. Similarly, dowsing is about training ourselves to be constantly attentive to our intuitive senses.

My years of being a composer gave me intimate experience with the multi-dimensional realms because I journeyed there routinely to envision my compositions. When I began to dowse, I entered the Dowsing Mind very quickly because it was quite similar to the changes of consciousness that I experienced when I was composing.

Your experiences will be different. It is important that we use all of our individual skills as we dowse. Which of your five senses is the most highly developed? Are you primarily a seeing person, a touching person, a hearing person, or even a "fragrance" person? How can you use that honed awareness to improve your dowsing? You will find that your senses become more sensitive when you change your consciousness and enter the Dowsing Mind. Be aware of that shift and allow it to develop. In that way you will be improving your dowsing.

Story Time Again

Okay, now that you have practiced the experiments for finding and following fault lines and other items, I'll entertain you with another story.

My wife, Elyn, and I were traveling in the British Isles. We were following various "signs" or "indications" of Elen of the Ways, an ancient, northern European reindeer goddess who is usually represented by the figure of a woman with reindeer antlers attached to (or growing from) her head. During a meditation, Elyn had received an invitation from Elen of the Ways, who "said," "Follow my Sarn Helen routes in Wales and I'll show you what happens!" When Elyn told this to me, I immediately agreed we should go and see what lay in store for us.

A few weeks later, we traveled from Spain (where we were living) to Wales, where we met our friend/guide Ros Briagha, who knows a great deal about ancient ways and paths. Our first goal was to walk the ancient Roman and pre-Roman roads in Wales that are called Sarn Helen (Helen's Ways). Some of these are still marked on official Ordinance Survey maps. Though most of the roads have been obliterated or paved over with modern highways, there are a few places where they can still be walked.

We were driving on a local highway, enroute to a still-extant section of Sarn Helen that Ros knew about. As we whizzed by, Elyn (notice the similarity: Elyn, Elen, Helen) spotted a roadside sign advertising "Sarn Helen Café." She told Ros we had to go there and Ros agreed. So we turned around and drove into the tiny village of Coelbryn, the reputed birthplace of St. Patrick. We drove through the village on a street named Sarn Helen but didn't find Sarn Helen Café.

When we reached the end of the street, we found a small memorial park. On the pavement were two large, detailed, mosaic maps that showed the Sarn Helen roads in Wales. Between the maps was a path that went up the hill from where we were standing. It was our first encounter with Sarn Helen! We walked up the hill and back to fulfill a part of our agreement to walk on Elen's Ways in Wales.

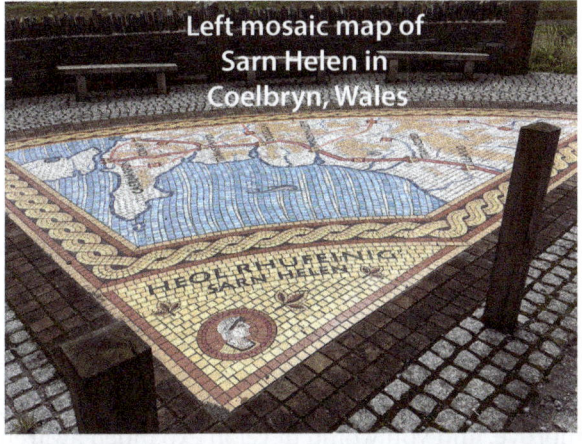

Left mosaic map of Sarn Helen in Coelbryn, Wales

Right mosaic map of Sarn Helen in Coelbryn, Wales (Ros Briagha standing on the map) Sarn Helen ways

Sarn Helen leading away from the mosaic maps

Ros was flabbergasted. She said that she had driven that road countless times and had never noticed the sign for Sarn Helen Café. Nor had she driven into that tiny village and seen the mosaic maps. Coincidence? Synchronicity? Dowsing for Sarn Helen without rods? You be the judge. I'll entertain you with more of our adventures on Elen's Ways later in the book. For now, just keep on dowsing!

If you were to stop reading this book right now and just continue to practice what you have learned, you could develop into a very good dowser. Your Dowsing Mind would gradually improve, and you would develop expanded awareness of the world around you and your relationship with it.

In future sections I will provide more ways for you to refine your dowsing techniques. Later, we will dive into some very deep esoteric waters. Take your time and continue to enjoy the ride if you choose—or just be satisfied with practicing what you have learned so far.

Further Information about Dowsing Tools

We have used very simple tools to learn dowsing, but you may want to explore some commercially available tools. Just remember that a tool is just a tool, and *you* are the dowser. Nevertheless, looking at all the available devices can be fun, and you may find one or more that you really like to work with.

First, let's talk about pendulums. There are thousands out there in all shapes and sizes, with chains and cords of every description, from solid gold to cotton string. The shape can vary from a simple pyramid to a cone to an elaborate, multi-layered gizmo. The weight at the end can be made from precious or semi-precious stone, metal, wood, etc. People who are attracted to crystals and gemstones often have preferences for one mineral over another. You may find some difference between various crystals, so test them and see what you feel.

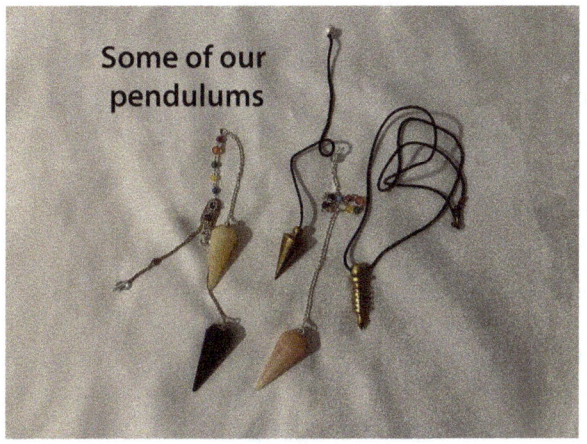

Some of our pendulums

I know a gemologist who prefers black tourmaline and clear quartz for pendulums and uses them for specific kinds of dowsing. I have also seen on the internet a super-macho cowboy type who uses (and sells) pendulums made out of rifle shells. Whatever turns you on! The point being, try them out and make a choice that makes you comfortable. Go to your local New Age bookstore/gift shop or a local gem/mineral shop and see what they have for sale. Move into your Dowsing Mind and see what information you get before you make your purchase. You can buy your pendulum online, but it is best if you can "feel" the energy in person.

Whatever material you choose for your pendulum, it is important to take proper care of it. You will need to cleanse it of old, stale energy, just as you would cleanse yourself after working in the garden. Water and salt are generally recommended for cleaning crystals. Some minerals do just fine with these substances, but others will be damaged. Ask the person selling you the pendulum how to care for it. Or find a person who is knowledgeable about minerals to guide you. You can also look online for advice about the care of minerals and crystals.

Your pendulum is an important tool and should be properly cared for and stored carefully. Small leather or silk bags are ideal for storing your pendulum. They fit easily into a pocket or purse and offer protection from unwanted contamination or damage. The silk may even help contain the crystal's energy.

A good universal tool that is safe for cleaning all crystals is an open, horizontal amethyst geode with a flattish basin on which you can place your crystals. We have such a geode, and we place our crystals on it when they need cleaning. We take them to an open area where the crystals can be cleaned by sunlight, starlight, and moonlight, and they are energetically clean in a day or two. Don't forget to clear your geode from time to time as well.

Amethyst geode for clearing crystals

Crystals being cleared on the amethyst geode

As for L-rods, there are many variations and a variety of materials to choose from. My wife, Elyn, has a pair of rods that are made from 100-year-old copper telegraph lines. She purchased them when we were traveling in Ireland. We were intrigued by the idea that the copper had been used for many years as a communications medium. That seemed absolutely appropriate to us.

I use a pair of telescoping L-rods that fold down so small that I can hide them in my hand. These rods are quite useful for dowsing in churches and temples. Since I don't want to disturb worshippers and priests, I can keep them hidden. Priests (and tourism officials!) sometimes take offense at people dowsing their sacred spaces, and they ask them to leave or to put away their tools. To avoid confrontations, I use my portable rods, and no one is the wiser.

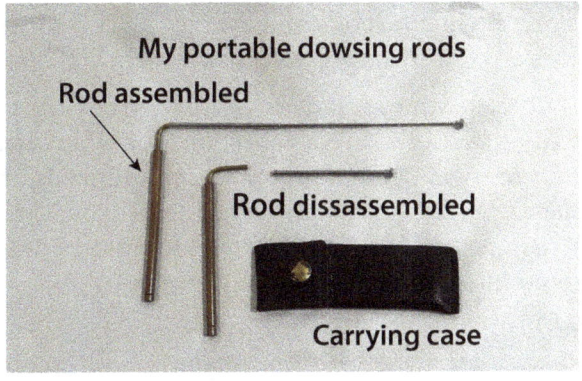

My portable dowsing rods
Rod assembled
Rod dissassembled
Carrying case

Most commercial L-rods have some sort of sleeve on the short part of the L so that the rods can turn freely. I find these sleeves very comfortable to hold, but, again, try them before buying them. In particular, make sure that the longer parts of the L's are not too long. If they are too long and get in each other's way, you can simply cut them down to a more comfortable size. Remember that rods are tools, not magical devices, but you do need them to be long enough to have some weight or they won't work well. Weight and balance are important and quite individual, so try them out and spend some time with them before committing to make them your own. When you have the right pair of rods in your hands, they will feel right.

Some high-tech rods have complicated springs or other devices that look wonderful but may or may not appeal to you. I've even seen one that has detachable parts for inserting a sample of the substance you want to dowse for. Just remember: it is your intention that is important. These devices probably work because they are an aid to your own mental process. I'm willing to entertain the notion that having a sample of the substance attached to your rods might "attract" that substance, but that is only speculation. More likely, it helps your inner dowsing sense attune to the frequency of what you are looking for. I will have a lot more to say about this subject later in the book when I talk about resonance.

In summary, the dowsing tools you use are a very personal preference. Buying several can be a nice reward to yourself for the new skill-set you are acquiring.

I know dowsers who use only one set of rods or one pendulum, and others who have a collection. My wife, Elyn, and I have a variety of pendulums of different minerals, metals, and shapes. We each have one set of L-rods, and I am quite partial to my small, portable rods that can easily be hidden in (and sometimes disappear from) my pocket.

Do Those Fancy Devices Work?

Now I'm going to reveal a very deep secret. This alone is worth the price of this book, so listen up. Every fancy device you've ever seen and every dowsing chart[4] you've ever dowsed with your pendulum works, and they all work beautifully. I know that sounds like a contradiction to everything I've been saying, but it is true and I'm now going to reveal just how they all work.

If you believe in the efficacy of the device or the chart or whatever you are using, you will stop your analytic left brain from its usual activity and let the device do its thing. With the left brain out of the way, your Dowsing Mind goes to work and does what it does so well—revealing the things that it knows (and that YOU know on an intuitive level). So, if you can totally believe in some gadget, use it. Anything that will get the left brain out of the way will free up your Dowsing Mind. The information resides there, just waiting for you to discover it.

There. That's the deep, dark secret that is worth the price of this book. Reveal it only to your very closest friends. And don't let it keep you from using whatever tool you have been using to free up your Dowsing Mind. As I said before, dowsing tools are very personal devices, and you now know that they all work. So, go on believing in yourself and in your tools. They will stand you in good stead.

All dowsing devices work because they free up your Dowsing Mind and allow it to do its work. The devices are like training wheels on a bicycle. They are an aid until you don't need them anymore. So, continue to use whatever tools you like. I continue to use mine and they continue to work for me.

---

4   There are hundreds of charts that have been created to enable dowsers to get answers that go beyond the "yes" and "no" answers we have discussed. They are usually semi-circular or circular in form and have a number of areas that are labeled with words or numbers. Search for "Pendulum Dowsing Charts" online to view a sample of these charts.

Dowsing a chart with a pendulum

SAAMA, an Example in the Realm of Health

In 2016, while we were living in Girona, Spain, Elyn and I were trained in a healing technique called SAAMA. This technique enjoys considerable following in Spain and other Spanish-speaking countries. We were trained by Veturián Arana, the founder of this system. Vetu has developed an extensive set of diagnostic pie charts on which he lists every source of discomfort and disease that you can think of, both physical and psychological, along with alternative methods of treatment for these complaints. These numbered charts are coordinated by a master pie chart, which you dowse to determine which of the many charts you should concentrate on and in which order. The technique for choosing the chart and the particular sections of the chart is similar to the dowsing technique for using the Bovis scale[5] in dowsing. I will not detail the steps of this process, except to say that it provides many opportunities for the Dowsing Mind to be activated.

We have been favorably impressed with SAAMA as a diagnostic device and have used it ourselves from time to time. It works because it frees up the Dowsing Mind and allows

---

5   One of the more common pendulum-dowsing charts.

it to express itself in the areas of physical/emotional/mental health.

In cultures such as ours that denigrate the Dowsing Mind and intuitive senses in general, techniques like SAAMA are useful in establishing pathways into the inherent power of the human mind. Until we can fully embrace our own Dowsing Mind, these techniques will continue to be very useful.

Filters

As you go about your day, your mind is filled to overflowing with all the input from your physical sense organs. For example, concentrate for a few moments on your left big toe (or choose another one if you wish). Do it now. Don't just read about it. Close your eyes and find that toe. After a few seconds of concentrating, I'm betting you are aware of a whole bunch of sensations coming into your brain from that one small appendage on your foot. Do you have a feeling of pressure, some discomfort, an itch, a tingling sensation? Now shift your concentration to your right thumb. Feel anything? Of course you do! But did you feel it while you were concentrating on your toe? I'll bet your answer is "no."

Now consider all of your various body parts, including your arms, legs, torso, and head. The amount of physical sensation flooding into your brain at every moment staggers the imagination. Now consider the sensory input from what you see, hear, taste, and smell. It is clearly astounding and far beyond anyone's ability to process.

How do we deal with all this information? We filter out the vast majority and discard it. It is as if all that flood of data doesn't exist. In fact, the only way we manage to get through our day at all is by this vast filtering operation. Most modern Westerners are trained from an early age to concentrate on visual input, for the most part, and we only bring other sense organs into our attention when we need data from them. It hasn't always been that way—and still isn't in some indigenous cultures. So, what percentage of the available sense data are we usually aware of? Is 10% too much? 5%? Probably less than that.

Now, let's consider the sensory data coming in from our "sixth sense." You know about the sixth sense, or more accurately, senses. They are what we have been discussing in this book. Your Dowsing Mind gives you access to your sixth senses. They aren't sensed by the physical sense organs in your body. Most of us have been trained from an early age to ignore this sensory input entirely. We are told by "The People Who Know" (parents, teachers, etc.) that those senses don't exist. Well, we know now that they do and there is more than a single "sixth sense." Notice that we don't even have a good name for these senses except "extra-sensory." Our language describes the five physical senses, but we have to make up new words or use words intended for other purposes to even try to speak about the less tangible senses.

Where are those senses located, since they have no sense organs in our bodies? I will just say that you access these senses when you enter the Dowsing Mind. That is why we are making the effort to learn how to move into and out of the Dowsing Mind. We are becoming friends with those nonphysical senses and learning how to use them as we learn to dowse.

Dowsing in the Supermarket

Armed with your expertise in dowsing, take a trip to your local supermarket and see how dowsing for information can be helpful. I know, you don't want to be running up and down the aisles with your L-rods in hand, so you are going to need to develop some other techniques, which are variants on what I call "body dowsing" since you aren't using any tool other than your own body. The first I'll talk about is called muscle testing or applied kinesiology.

Experiment #9: Muscle Testing

Equipment needed: a packet of artificial sweetener and a friend to help you test.

Goal: learning to muscle test.

It has long been observed that your muscle strength diminishes in the presence of substances that are not good for your health. Here is a little experiment for you to try. You will need only two items for this experiment: a packet of artificial sweetener (aspartame or saccharine) and a friend to do the testing. Go to your kitchen and take down a packet of artificial sweetener. If you don't keep such items in your kitchen (good for you!), you can always pick up a packet the next time you are in a café, bar, or restaurant. You may be able to use a packet of sugar, but the results may not be as dramatic. Now recruit your friend for the experiment.

You are going to hold your arm extended either in front of you or out from your side. Your other arm is relaxed at your side. Your friend is going to try to push your arm down by pressing firmly on your wrist with his/her hand, and you are going to resist. Your friend doesn't need to try to break your arm—all that is needed is enough of a push to give an indication of how strong your arm muscles are when they are not being "challenged." That's your "base line."

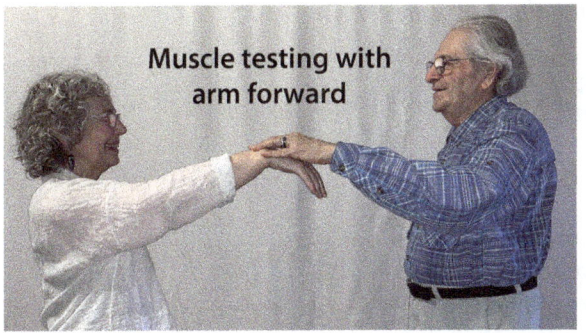
Muscle testing with arm forward

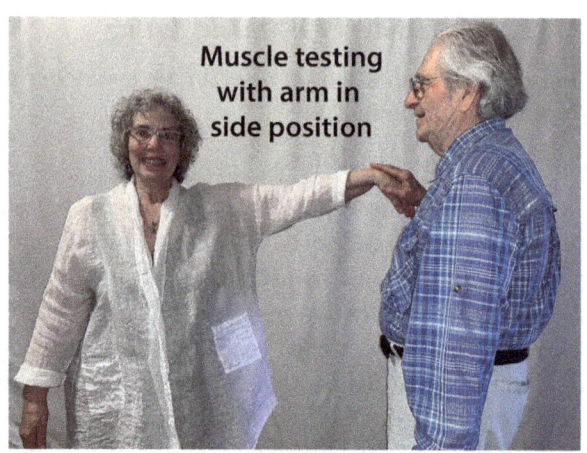

Next, put the packet of artificial sweetener in your other hand (the one down by your side) and place that hand on your stomach. Have your friend do the strength test again. Do you notice a difference in strength? Most people do.

Now trade places with your friend and test him/her. All you need to know is that strong means "yes" or positive, and weak means "no" or negative. In this case, a strong arm means "good for you" and a weaker arm means "bad for you." This is the information you will be seeking. By the way, you can try that same test with anything else you want—vitamins, sugar, chocolate, etc. Try it with something you know is good for you—and something you suspect isn't.

Experiment #10: And Now the Supermarket

Equipment needed: your local market and a friend to do the testing.

Goal: using muscle testing in a real-life situation.

You can use that slight difference in muscle strength to dowse for which products to buy in the supermarket. I'll detail the technique we use, or you can invent your own version. If we are in a natural foods grocery store (not Walmart or Kroger), Elyn and I will do the strength test openly. She will extend her arm and I will do the test.

First, we find out if Elyn's system is balanced. To do this, Elyn places her left foot slightly ahead of her right and extends her right arm. I check to see if she is strong by pressing down lightly on her hand or wrist. If I get "yes," she places her right foot slightly ahead of her left and extends her left arm. I check again to see if she is strong. If I get "yes," we go on to the next part of the test. If I get "no," I bring her into balance by gently rubbing the sensitive spots on the upper chest on either side of the sternum two inches or so below the v-shaped opening at the throat.

Rubbing the front points to restore balance

You will sense these places because they will feel slightly tender when you rub them. Then, if needed, I rub the corresponding locations on her back.

Rubbing the back points to restore balance

We test again to see if she is now strong. We almost always find that this rubbing exercise brings her into balance and she will now test strong.

Next we ask (silently or aloud) a series of questions, evaluating each one with the muscle test. Elyn asks, "Am I connected to Highest Source?" If we get "yes," she asks, "May we, can we, and should we ask these questions?" I test the strength of her arm as she says "may," "can," and "should." If we get "yes" on all of these questions, she's ready to begin dowsing for information about products. This takes only a few seconds once you get used to the routine.

A lot of valuable information is encapsulated in this series of questions, so I'll break it down.

- Highest Source. This is the central source of everything. You may call it God, Goddess, Great Spirit, the Void of Un-being, Universal Consciousness, or give it no name at all.
- May we? This is asking permission of the Highest Source to do this dowsing. Asking permission is central to everything we are doing, so we are making it overt here.
- Can we? This is asking if we have the ability to dowse for this at this time.
- Should we? This is asking if it is in our highest interest that we dowse for this at this time.

These are very important questions to ask. In fact, I would recommend that you ask something like this series of questions at the start of any dowsing session—whether for fault lines, vitamins, or whatever. You can add this to your dowsing routine from now on, and you will find that it increases the reliability of your results.

These questions and dowsing for the answers are a real help in shifting into the Dowsing Mind. And they serve to concentrate our attention on the process. We use them as a bridge to the Dowsing Mind.

After these preliminaries, Elyn holds a product (for example, a vitamin C supplement) in one hand against her belly, extends her other arm, and asks, "Is it in my highest interest to take this supplement now?" If we get "no" we don't buy it. If we get "yes," we may follow up with, "Is there another similar product (a different brand) in this store that would be better?" If we get "yes," we search for what product that might be. We also may ask questions like, "on a scale of 1-10, with 10 being the best, how good is this product for me?" Elyn's arm will be strong at the best number and weaker at the others.

Using this technique enables us to purchase the best products for our use. Of course, we don't do this for every purchase. We do it only if we are in doubt about what to buy. And we know that the answer is only good at that time. It's somewhat like taking a snapshot. Next week, Elyn may not need to take that supplement. We also dowse to find how much of the product to take (see p. 64).

If we are in Walmart or a similar store, or if Elyn is by herself, she will do a more discrete version of the test. She forms the thumb and forefinger (some people prefer the thumb and little finger) of each hand into a circle and links the two.

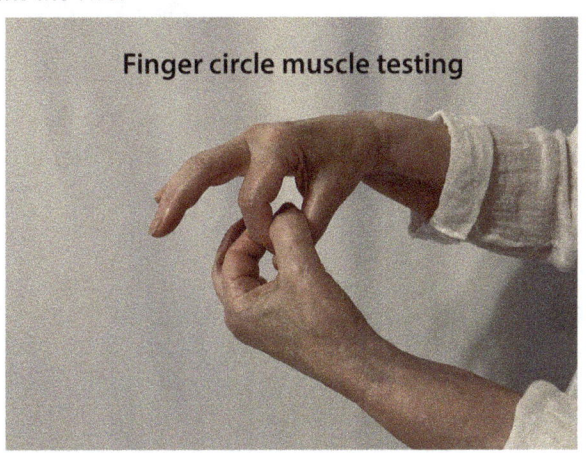

Finger circle muscle testing

She tests her muscle strength by trying to pull apart the finger circle of one hand by pulling one finger circle "through" that of the other. A strong circle means the product is a "yes" or good for her, and a weak circle means a "no" or not good for her. She asks the same list of questions as we do when doing the test above. It is fairly easy to tell if she is strong or weak in response.

An even more discrete version can be done with one hand. Place the second finger on top of the forefinger and push down. Again, you begin by determining your muscle strength or weakness. This will change depending on what is in your other hand. You can do this version of the test with your hand in a pocket, and no one will be the wiser!

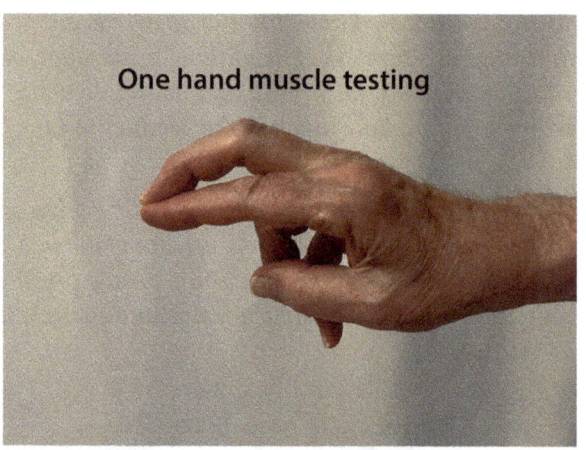

One hand muscle testing

If you have difficulty making this work, it could be that your good old left brain is getting in the way again and trying figure things out. Try going into your Dowsing Mind and see if it works better. You just have to be firm with your left brain in all these endeavors.

If you think this book is becoming a bit repetitious, well, it is. We are on a spiraling journey. I am gradually adding concepts when you are ready for them. You have to keep doing all these exercises over and over to become a good dowser. The best part is that all these versions of learning to trust your intuition work together to improve your dowsing abilities. If you use them all, you will be in Dowsing Mind frequently every day.

Remember:

- Check to see if your system is in balance. Rebalance if necessary.
- Ask permission (Am I connected to highest source? May I, can I, and should I ask these questions?).
- Go to your Dowsing Mind.
- Muscle-test by asking, "Is it in my highest interest to take this supplement (buy this product) now?"
- Check for muscle strength.
- If the response is not positive, try other products or don't purchase the product. Maybe you don't need it.
- Select your purchases on the basis of the results of the tests.

Expanding Beyond the Supermarket

You can apply the techniques you are learning for shopping in the supermarket to other decisions you need to make. We routinely dowse to choose products in stores and online. It has become our primary way of making such decisions. I can't claim that we have 100% accuracy with our dowsing, but my experience proves to me over and over that we make better decisions than we would have without dowsing.

If we are trying to choose a computer or a household appliance, we look at the available options, read reviews, narrow the choices to two or three that look good to us, and make the final choice by muscle testing. We will often ask if there is another item that will be better. If we get "yes," we widen our search.

And Now, Dowsing for Life

In recent years we have begun to use our dowsing techniques for major life decisions. We use the rods, muscle testing, and a technique we learned from Robert Moss called "sidewalk oracles" whenever we have an important decision to make (Moss, *Sidewalk Oracles: Playing with Signs, Symbols, and Synchronicity in Everyday Life*, 2015). Moss describes how we can use an overheard snatch of conversation, a roadside sign, or a newspaper headline to give us information on our best course of action. Relying on sidewalk oracles is a very useful—and entertaining—form of dowsing.

I will have more examples to report in Part Two, but I will illustrate here how we used sidewalk oracles and dowsing to negotiate the beginning of the 2020 Covid-19 pandemic.

A Walkabout in the USA

We had moved to Spain in 2008 to explore the expat life. It was there that we began to write our series of guidebooks on sacred sites in Europe, called "Powerful Places in . . .".

Our Powerful Places book series

In September 2019, Elyn received an email from Eileen Nauman in Arizona, USA, inviting her to visit her to learn Native American shamanic ways of walking the land. Eileen had watched an interview with Elyn on the Ancient-Origins Premium channel (https://www.ancient-origins.net/), and she had visited our Powerful Places website. Eileen was intrigued with our books and wanted to show us a different perspective. Our emphasis had been on European sites, which are usually buildings, standing stones, monuments, or other works of humans. This is the natural result of tens-of-thousands of years of dense human habitation of the European continent and the penchant of Europeans for building stone monuments on their sites of power. On the other hand, Native Americans, however, usually honor their sacred sites in nature and the naturally powerful places on the land by *not* building on them.

When Elyn read the invitation, we did what we usually do with everything new that comes our way—we dowsed to see how to respond. The response was a strong "yes," so we accepted this as our next "walkabout" assignment. We made plans to spend the month of December 2019 working with Eileen. I thought this would be a perfect opportunity for me to practice my dowsing skills in a new setting.

Arriving in Arizona, I felt an immediate sense of being home. The town of Cottonwood was like the small Kansas town I grew up in, except for the mountains and amazing red rock formations all around.

Sedona´s famed red rock formations drew us back to the USA

I felt comfortable in a way that I had not for many years living in Spain. Before the first week passed, we were thinking about returning to the USA for the next part of our lives. We met a number of people with whom we felt connected, and the clerks in the stores were easy to make small talk with. I told Elyn that they even understood my sense of humor, which made me very happy. (Little did I realize that rampant racism and sexism were also a part of the familiarity I felt with the place. This gave me an opportunity to confront the lingering unconscious racism and sexism I still carry around with me. But that's another story—see my www.Fandango.com blog if you're interested.)

It wasn´t long before we began to make plans for returning to the USA. We knew we would need to sever our eleven years of connections in Spain, including housing, phones, internet, health care, etc. Eileen (a skilled astrologer) urged us not to travel in the month of January 2020 because of her astrological readings, so we decided to postpone our return to Oviedo, Spain, until mid-February. That would also give us time to prepare the state-side aspects of our move.

Our new friends were very helpful, and by February 1 we were living in a rented house in Cottonwood, which we furnished with basic furniture and kitchenware, and we had leased a car. We negotiated the crazy US health insurance system and established phone and internet service. We could now return to Spain and clear up our affairs there. Finding and buying all we needed was aided greatly by our usual dowsing techniques. It is amazing how much easier decisions are when you dowse for guidance.

As soon as we had decided to move back to the US, Elyn contacted an expat couple we had met briefly in Oviedo, and we learned that they were planning to move there. They were very happy to take over our apartment lease and were interested in purchasing some of our furniture and goods. We planned to return to Spain in mid-February, and we thought we would have a until mid-March to complete our move from Spain. But this couple suddenly needed to have an Oviedo address by March 1 to complete their application for Spanish residency. That gave us only 10 days to return to Spain, sort and pack, and move out of our apartment.

The view of the cathedral from our apartment in Oviedo, Spain

Elyn thought about asking the couple for more time, but when we dowsed, we got a clear "no." The Covid-19 pandemic was by now on the horizon but had not yet hit in earnest. We purchased face masks as a preventative before flying back to Spain. Elyn and a dear friend in Oviedo went into high gear with packing, and the movers came to ship our stuff to the US on February 28. The other couple moved into our apartment March 1, and we moved into a hotel while we finished up details of disentangling from Spain.

We had thought that we might spend several weeks traveling in Spain and Portugal to see my daughter and her husband (who live in southern Spain) and to visit several sacred sites we had been wanting to see. But when we dowsed, none of these plans seemed good. The Covid-19 outbreak was beginning to look like a growing problem, but we didn't know how big it would be. We asked when we should return to the US and dowsed several alternative dates. We got a strong "yes" that the time was RIGHT NOW. So we scheduled our return flight the US as soon as possible—March 9. Although we didn't know it when we made our plans, it turned out that date was just five days before air travel was practically shut down between Europe and the US because of the Covid-19 pandemic.

We made it back to the US without problem. When the airport shuttle dropped us off at our rented house in Cottonwood, Arizona, we put ourselves into 14-day self-isolation while we waited to see if we had contracted the Covid-19 virus. Because of our earlier planning, we had a house that was ready to live in and even had supplies of food and other necessities.

Looking back, I see that every step of our moving process, informed by dowsing, had enabled us to ride out the initial Covid-19 pandemic in relative safety and comfort in the US. We felt that we had been guided every step of the way using our dowsing skills, even though we could not have understood or anticipated the reason for each of our decisions. For example, had we not taken the additional time initially to set up housekeeping in Arizona, we would not have been able to return to an already comfortably set-up house. Had the American couple not needed our apartment in Oviedo by March 1st, and had we not decided after dowsing to forego further travel, we would have been stuck in Spain for the duration of the crisis. We are very grateful for the skills that we employed in making this move. Perhaps our dowsing skills had even saved our lives—or at least our health.

It remains to be seen if this move to Cottonwood is a long-term move or just another stop on our walkabout. Only time will tell. We remain ready to move on when the time is right.

Asking Questions Precisely

In dowsing for information, it is always important to state your questions in a way that can receive a clear "yes" or "no" answer. In our experience, when dowsing gives us spurious results it is because we have not asked the question clearly enough or haven't asked all the relevant questions. With this in mind, I will summarize some of the questions we asked ourselves in the process of making the decision to return to the USA.

- Should we stay for more than one month in the USA at this time? Yes.
- Should I write a book on dowsing while we are here? Yes.
- Should we relocate from Spain to Cottonwood, Arizona, at this time? Yes.
- Should we buy a house in Cottonwood, Arizona, now? No.
- Should we rent this house in Cottonwood, Arizona? Yes.
- Should we buy this specific mattress for our house in Cottonwood? Yes.
- Etc., etc.

Clarity is essential. For example, if we had asked, "Should we relocate from Spain to the US?" We might have gotten a "yes," but the "when" wouldn't be clear. The answer could have been "yes, but not now." Be very careful to make your questions clear and through so you will get more accurate results. You can also check your answers by couching the questions in different ways. For example, we might have asked, "Is Cottonwood, Arizona, the very best place for us to live now?" or "Is this the best time for us to leave Spain and return to the US?" This process is called double-checking and it is highly recommended. And remember, the answer is specific to the time when you are asking. Like a computer, dowsing answers are only as good (and accurate) as the information entered—in this case, the question asked. When the external situation changes, so might the response.

A recent example will serve to emphasize the importance of asking the right questions. We were dowsing to find which of several nutritional supplements Elyn should take. Here is the response we got:

- "Is this product good for me today?" Yes.
- "Is this product bad for me today?" Yes.
- "On a scale of 1 to 10, how good is it for me today? (Count down from 10 to 1, testing with each number.)
- "On a scale of 1 to 10, how bad is it for me today? (count down from 10 to 1, testing with each number.)

That had us stumped until we asked another question:

- "Are there side effects of this supplement that are not in Elyn's best interest?" Yes.

Elyn has had similar results when muscle-testing about chocolate and coffee, a mix of "yes" and "no," good and bad.

Sometimes we get "no" for both good and bad, when the effect of the product is neutral. Asking the right questions and double-checking your responses is mandatory in all information dowsing.

Also check to see that you are programming the rods accurately when you are dowsing. Telling the rods how to respond and being quite specific about what you are seeking makes for more accurate readings.

Determining Proper Dosage

We use dowsing to determine the proper dosage of supplements we take daily. If we have established a proper dosage, we may or may not check every day. The process is quite simple if we are using muscle testing. We ask the question, "Is it in my highest interest to take this supplement today? If "yes," we ask how much. We generally choose a number slightly higher than we believe is right. Then we muscle test and lower the number until we get a "yes." For example:

- It is in my highest interest to take 5 of this supplement today. If "no"—
- It is in my highest interest to take 4 of this supplement today. If "no"—
- It is in my highest interest to take 3 of this supplement today. Continue to count down until you get a "yes" answer.

If we get a number that we feel doubtful about, we may try again, starting with "0" and counting up. Use your good judgment with this and avoid overdosing on supplements.

Disclaimer: We are in no way suggesting that you use dowsing in lieu of seeking and/or following medical advice. We are not responsible for your decisions. Feel free to make this process your own by tweaking it to make yourself more comfortable. Revise or choose a completely different strategy.

Dowsing for the Depth of Water

Given what you've learned, you can now easily see how to dowse for the depth of water when you are dowsing on the land. You can ask a series of "yes" and "no" questions and get the answers from your rods. For example:

- Is the water at 10 feet depth? (No)
- Is the water at 20 feet depth? (No)
- Is the water between 50 and 100 feet? (yes)
- Is the water between 100 and 90 feet? (No)

Continue until you get a "yes" response, and that will be the approximate depth of the water.

It´s Practice Time

You now have a huge new treasure trove of information and techniques to practice. I recommend that you spend considerable time working with these new tools. The rewards may include better choices at the supermarket, better use of your financial resources, better ways of making decisions, and better health. Take time to make muscle-testing your own. You don't need to do it exactly as Elyn and I do it. Create your own version—one that works for you and feels comfortable.

If you stop reading this book right now and just continue to practice, you will find that dowsing, both in the field and for information, comes easier and easier, and decision-making can be a lot of fun. I hope that our story about how we negotiated the initial part of the Covid-19 pandemic will encourage you to try these techniques for yourself.

Remember that dowsing puts you in Dowsing Mind. And keep in mind that time and space work differently there. Time may slow down, speed up, or even stop while you dowse. Coming back from the Dowsing Mind can be a bit disorienting. I sometimes feel a bit dizzy. Several deep, grounding breaths will help you with reorientation.

The Next Part of Our Elen of the Ways Adventure

I left off with our "Elen of the Ways Adventure" in Wales with our finding the mosaic maps showing Sarn Helen ways in a small rural village. Our adventure continued, taking us to Ireland, Scotland, the Orkney Isles, and back to Wales, following our intuition, dowsing, and looking for guidance from "sidewalk oracles." As I mentioned in the previous section, the term "sidewalk oracles" comes from our active-dreaming teacher, the prolific writer Robert Moss, and his book *Sidewalk Oracles: Playing with Signs, Symbols, and Synchronicity in Everyday Life.*

So, back to our journey. We followed the guidance of Elen of the Ways as we made our way across Wales. We let the trip unfold without advanced planning. This was very instructive for me. I have been a planner for most of my life. I like to scope out the road ahead and make extensive plans—and then prepare contingency plans in case the first plans don't pan out. Having a Plan A, Plan B, C, D, . . . has been my preferred way of moving through life. Letting Elen of the Ways be our guide taught me to let go of all that (well, not completely, but it was a start). Notice that "planning" is a left-brain activity, and "letting it unfold" is a Dowsing Mind activity. This is important!

About two weeks into our adventure, Elyn and I were sitting in the airport in Edinburgh, Scotland, waiting for a flight to the Orkney Isles. We fell into an intense, soul-searching conversation. Was this trip just a random walk? Were the sidewalk oracles, the signs and symbols we saw every day that we were using to guide us—were these just figments of our overactive imaginations? Were we drawing lines between dots that were really just unrelated dots? Were we making connections between signs and symbols that just weren't there? Were we crazy—or just foolish—to be spending our time and money in this silly way?

Upset and unsettled, Elyn took a walk down the airport concourse and, as she is wont to do, picked up a batch of free brochures and magazines from a display rack to wile away the time before our flight. She returned, handed me a magazine, and then sat down to peruse the rest of her collection. I took one look at the cover of the magazine and gasped. Guess what was on the cover? A collage of an antler-headed woman—Elen of the Ways!

Elyn of the Ways cover image

I showed the magazine to Elyn, who hadn't even looked at the magazine when she picked it up. There, in front of our eyes, was visual proof that our adventure was not a random walk and that Elen of the Ways was truly guiding us every step of the way. Inside was an interview with the cover artist. He said that he had always been inspired by antler-headed goddesses.

Just when we were in the most doubt about our venture, Elen of the Ways came through in tangible form to tell us to keep the faith. A framed copy of that magazine cover is pinned on Elyn's bulletin board.

Summary

Before we launch into deeper territories, I'll provide a general summary of the steps to follow in preparation for dowsing. As I've said several times, dowsing is a very personal matter. You need to make it your own. It is important that you develop regular habits for entering and leaving the dowsing realm.

Remember:

- Check to see if your internal energetic system is in balance. Rebalance if necessary.
- Ask permission (Am I connected to Highest Source? May I, can I, and should I ask these questions?).
- State what you are seeking in clear, unambiguous terms.
- Go to your Dowsing Mind and shift your state of awareness.
- Place the rods or pendulum in search position.
- Begin dowsing.
- When you get a sign that you have found what you are looking for, double-check by approaching from a different direction or asking the question in a different way.

Part Two

As I mentioned in Part One, we are on a spiraling path in this book. Your primary task will be to use your dowsing skills in as many areas of your life as you are inclined to do so. I will be adding some techniques as we go along, but the primary focus in the three sections that follow will be to introduce you to ever-deeper areas of your inner being. Part Two concentrates on a fuller discussion of the multi-dimensional realms. In Part Three we will look at the cosmos and you as energetic phenomena, and in Part Four we will explore the nature of consciousness. There will be many opportunities for you to deepen your dowsing practice as you pursue these more esoteric areas, and from time to time I will share stories from my life that will show you how I use my dowsing skills.

How I Discovered the Multi-Dimensional Realms

Before we take a deeper dive into dowsing, I will tell you how I discovered the multi-dimensional realms.

In my earlier life, from my early 20s through late 50s, I was a professional composer and textbook author. I was Professor of Music Theory and Composition at Iowa State University for over 28 years. During that time I wrote approximately 150 compositions and 6 university-level music-theory textbooks. I prepared myself for this career by visiting the multi-dimensional realms.

When I spontaneously began to compose music as an 8-year-old child, it came without effort. But when I was an undergraduate music student at the University of Kansas, I was contemplating making composing my life work. I felt I needed to call on sources of creativity beyond those provided by my usual environment.

By "chance," I came across a small paperback book that promised to teach me self-hypnosis. I read the instructions carefully. Every day I would spend a few minutes putting myself into a trance and then try to create a piece of music. To my surprise, I was quite successful, and the musical ideas flowed more easily. I had discovered a secret key to creativity!

The self-hypnosis technique became my standard method for beginning a session of composing, and I guarded it closely, telling no one what I was doing. My teachers didn't care how I composed the music. They were only concerned with the quality of my production.

The self-hypnosis technique served me quite well, and I completed my undergraduate degree in music composition. I gradually expanded the technique to include using dreamtime for creative work. Before retiring at night, I would spend a few minutes reviewing a composition I was working on. I would go over it in my mind, leaving off at the point I had reached that day. Although I would be looking at the music notation during this process, I would be hearing the music in my head. When I went to sleep, my mind would continue to be quite active. The music I was composing filled my mind and would extend beyond its current end point. Sometimes I would see a dreamtime ensemble performing the piece, but other times it was simply the music itself that I heard.

I found that I could easily continue the composition the next morning when I awoke, and I would have a good idea of what its future direction should be. In case you are wondering about my ability to "hear" music in my head, professional musicians are trained to do this in "ear training" courses. Everyone has this ability to some extent. Have you ever had a tune "stuck in your head?" It plays over and over until you wish you could dismiss it. That is "hearing" music in your head.

These hypnotic and dreamtime techniques gave me access to a source of creative ideas that enabled me to complete a Master's degree and finally a Ph.D. in music composition. During all those years, I kept my creative process to myself and revealed it to no one. I sometimes wondered if I had been awake most of the night, but I would get up in the morning rested and be able to work for the entire day. I did this night after night with no ill effects for years. It was only when I studied Active Dreaming with Robert Moss (Moss, *Active Dreaming,* 2011) that it became clear to me that I was actually in a lucid-dreaming state during the night.

A lucid dream is one where the person dreaming is aware that they are dreaming. They may even be able to influence the course of the dream, acting as a sort of "theater director" of the dream.

A natural extension of the lucid-dreaming technique is using daytime naps for creative purposes. The results are equally effective. Self-hypnosis, meditation, dreaming, lucid dreaming, and daydreaming are all ways of accessing the multi-dimensional realms. When I began writing music-theory textbooks, and, later, our "Powerful Places" guidebook series, I used the techniques I had honed during years of composing to imagine the content and layout of these books.

One of my music textbooks

In short, I have used the multi-dimensional realm creatively for much of my adult life. And, by the way, the contents of this book were created from there.

Later, when I was a university professor teaching young people to compose music, I developed several techniques that would not seem as "far out" as self-hypnosis and dreaming for evoking the creative muse. For example, I would tell my students to imagine, as clearly as possible, the first performance of their work. They were to visualize the musicians coming on stage and the audience awaiting the performance. The more vividly they could imagine this scene, the more successful they would be in hearing the music. The musicians would get ready and the performance would begin. I would emphasize that the students must listen very carefully at this moment, because they would always hear music in their minds. They needed to get as much as possible of this music down on paper. For example, what was the tempo of the music? What melody, harmony, or rhythm did they hear? Typically, there was not much that they could capture at first, but I assured them that with practice they would get better at it. (Just like dowsing!)

These fragments were the beginning of the composition they would create. Later they could determine if that was really where the piece should begin or if it needed an introduction. Was this the first movement of the piece or a later movement? These considerations could be thought through consciously, using what the student knew about the theory and structure of music (engaging the left brain). I could guide them through this process with discussion and suggestions. The visualization technique put the student into an altered state of consciousness where the creative process could begin in the multi-dimensional realm.

The basic idea is the following: the original creative material came from the realm beyond the analytic mind, and the student learned to draw on the multi-dimensional realms as the source of ideas. (Elyn suggests perhaps they were time-traveling into the future, hearing a piece they hadn't yet composed in the present. That explanation also seems reasonable to me.) Switching off the conscious analytic mind (left brain) comes easily to some, but others require methods and techniques to get there. Some artists visit the imaginal realms with the aid of drugs, but I never needed chemicals to enter these realms.

A few years ago, when I wrote a piece about my creative process for my online FandangoLife.com blog, a friend who is a very creative electrical engineer posted a response saying that he did all his circuit-design work in the multi-dimensional realms. The multi-dimensional realms contain much more than the materials for artistic creation. Witness Einstein's theory of relativity.

Elyn is a writer and fiber artist, and she relies on images and information coming from the multi-dimensional realm(s). She has coined the term "imaginaut" for those of us who do our work there. She says she gets visual "downloads" that she then puts into words. Some of the novels she has written include people who later showed up in real life, and they contain information that she didn't know at the time she was writing. Her fiber-art figures have come to her from the imaginal realms as well.

Please remember that the multi-dimensional realms are neither imaginary nor fantasy. They are as real as the 3-D world, but in a different way. People speak of Dreamtime, the imaginal realms, the Council of Elders, the Afterlife, Heaven, the faery realms, the Akashic records, the Inner Convocation, the Underworld, and many other locations in the multi-dimensional universe. Some of these areas have been more explored than others, but no one knows or can know the whole map of these territories. Your Dowsing Mind gives you access to one small corner of this vast terrain.

What is generally true of all multi-dimensional states—including dreaming—is that they are out-of-body experiences. I project my consciousness out of the physical limits of my body. It may appear that I am pre-occupied since I am absent from consciousness on the physical plane, but I'm wide awake in the imaginal realm! As Robert Moss points out repeatedly, the state between waking and sleeping, called the "hypnogogic" state, can be used creatively. I will be suggesting some exercises later that will help you to enter into the imaginal realm in the hypnogogic state.

Being in the imaginal realms is not strange or unusual. We all spend considerable time in the imaginal realms when we sleep, whether we remember our dreams or not. Humans and many other animals require sleep to keep their nervous systems healthy. Sleep deprivation results in severe psychological problems and even psychosis, but we aren't talking about sleep deprivation. You might call it "sleep enrichment."

Imaginauts use the imaginal realms for creative work, bringing the results through to waking consciousness and manifesting them on the physical plane (the 3-D world). I like to say that I am not just a tourist in the multi-dimensional realms, I have been a business traveler there for most of my life!

Where Is the Multi-Dimensional World?

As you are learning, the multi-dimensional world is enormous and multi-faceted. It is a magical kingdom where you can gather creative ideas and information that you can bring back into 3-D reality. What you create or find there can have a major impact in the wider world, and you can deposit the profits in your bank account. Believe me: Many have become rich that way! That should be enough incentive to keep you practicing.

Where is the multi-dimensional realm? For that, we will need to look into folklore and history a bit. Traditional Celtic people have a place they call the Land of Eternal Youth or the Other World. They say that this is an underworld, or a world out at sea. This world for them is located near the middle (or 3-D) world, but it can't be found by simply digging into the earth. They sometimes call it the *Tír na nÓg*, a place where a race of supernatural beings is said to reside. They also talk about "thin" places or places where the veil between the worlds is permeable at actual physical locations, and sometimes at certain times of the year like Halloween. Many other cultures have similar places associated with landscape features such as mountains, rivers, islands, caves, and seas.

Other places in the multi-dimensional realms have no physical access point. There is said to be a library called the Akashic Records, a record of everything that has happened in the 3-D world. But it is not located in this 3-D world at all. There's also the Council of the Elders, the Inner Convocation, and many more "locations." Places with no physical, 3-D existence are located in the imaginal—not imaginary—realms.

Camille Flammarion, *L' atmosphère: météorologie populaire* (Paris: Hachette, 1888, p. 163.)

Time in Multi-Dimensional Space

Another feature of the multi-dimensional realms is that time works differently there. R. J. Stewart, who is an expert on Celtic and faery lore, says, "Time cycles within the faery world are different from ours. The commonly reported theme is that a short period of time in the faery realm may be centuries in the human world" (Stewart, *Earth Light,* 1992, p. 35). The short story "Rip Van Winkle" by Washington Irving illustrates this theme. Rip Van Winkle, the main character in the story, finds himself in a remote place with a group of men wearing antiquated Dutch clothing. He drinks some of their liquor and falls asleep. When he awakes, he discovers that his gun is rusted and rotting, and his beard is a foot long. When he returns to his village, he discovers that 20 years have passed, and his young children are now grown men and women.

Time in the multi-dimensional realms can also be stretched, allowing longer periods of time there to be shorter times in the 3-D realm. In other areas of the multi-dimensional realms, time may not exist at all and everything is static. Robert Moss says that we can move back and forward in time in these imaginal realms, but that's another topic.

The Multi-Dimensional Realms and Dowsing

In the beginning, when you paused the left brain and went to your "blank" space, you were sensing into a part of the multi-dimensional realms where you could access your Dowsing Mind.

You may have been told by your parents or your teachers that you were an idle daydreamer for spending time in the multi-dimensional realm. I know I was. "Earth to Gary!" they would say. Well, they were just wrong, that's all, because I learned to bring back the riches of the multi-dimensional realms into the 3-D world. I became a published composer, a music textbook author, and more.

I'll say it another way: An idle daydreamer is a person who comes back from the multi-dimensional realms empty handed. A person who comes back bearing gifts and treasure is called a creative thinker, a creative artist, or even a creative genius. All creatives have been travelers in the multi-dimensional realms. Believe me, you can be one of those people.

A Deeper Dive into Dowsing

And now, for a deeper dive into dowsing. First, a warning: If you have been reading this book and not doing the exercises regularly, you are going to find the following sections harder going. In fact, you may think I have taken leave of my senses and you may feel like tossing the book. If so, so be it. But if you are willing to take the time and practice all the previous exercises, you will find what I am about to say makes better sense.

Take a look around you. Look at the air. OK, I know that the air is transparent and can't be seen unless it is filled with dust, and that's still not the air, it's the dust. So, just imagine that you can see it. It looks pretty empty, doesn't it? Now imagine turning on a radio. Instantly, you have a choice of many channels, including numerous styles of music, the news, and talk shows. Where do those signals come from? They are in the air all around you all the time, even though you can't see them. Now imagine turning on a TV set. Depending on your cable or satellite contract, you have a huge selection of channels. Turn on your computer and connect with the WIFI server in your house. You can read numerous emails that are directed to you and you alone. All these signals travel through that so-called empty air, along with the signals for everyone else's emails. Turn on your GPS and you can find the location of a store in your town and even know exactly where you are on the planet.

All this information is beamed to you through that "empty" air from satellites passing overhead and from nearby cell-phone towers. These signals and many more that I haven't mentioned fill the air all around us every second of the day and night. Look at the list of available servers on your cell phone, and you'll see a small sample of what I'm talking about. Many frequency bands are available if you have the proper receiver. It is all a matter of tuning the receiver to the proper frequency. And those are just the signals that are generated by humans using our amazing technology!

The range of signals coming in from the multi-dimensional realms is even vaster than all the human-created signals. You've been using some of these signals in your previous dowsing experiments, even though I haven't mentioned it. But there are many more channels available to you just for the asking. Well, you may have to do a little work! You have the proper receiver (intuitive senses) for some of these channels built into your nervous system, thanks to your ancient ancestors. But there are more receivers that you can access with further work. This is where we are going, so hold on to your hat!

Prelude to Multi-Dimensional Sight

In the 5th-century BCE, the Greek philosopher Empedocles presented a theory of how eyesight works. He said the eyes were like lanterns that beamed out a special kind of light. He said that sight was the result of the light of our eyes touching whatever we looked at. Certain particles go forth from the eye to meet particles given forth from the object, and the resultant contact constitutes vision. Later researchers repudiated Empedocles and said that the eyes were merely receptors of the light that came to them.

But recently it has been discovered that the eyes do, indeed, produce some slight but measurable light. Perhaps that light from the eyes can account for the often-observed phenomenon where you sense someone is looking at you even though your back is turned. As Humphery Bogart said to Ingrid Bergman in the 1942 film "Casablanca," "Here's lookin' at you, kid!"

The Sufis (Islamic mystics) have long acknowledged the power of the glance. The 20th-century Sufi teacher Hazrat Inayat Khan said, "I mourned in love and pierced the hearts of men; And when my fiery glance fell on the rocks, the rocks burst forth as volcanoes" (Khan, *The Dance of the Soul: Gayan Vadan Nirtan,* 2007).

The pineal gland, which is buried deep in the human brain and in the brains of most vertebrates, is considered to be an atrophied photoreceptor. In some species of amphibians and reptiles, the pineal is linked to a light-sensing organ known as the parietal eye or the third eye. This third eye is represented by the spot that many people in India apply to their foreheads just above their eyebrows. It also symbolizes the brow chakra, and there may be a relationship between the 6th chakra and the pineal gland. All these manifestations of sight show that what and how we see is more complicated than we were taught.

In the old Superman and Superwoman comics, the superheroes have x-ray vision. It is portrayed in the comics as a force emanating from the eyes or just above the eyes. Perhaps the latter indicates the third eye or pineal gland. Google "x-ray vision" to see a selection of comic images. Superman may view the multi-dimensional realms when he turns on his x-ray vision. Perhaps the creators of the Superman and Superwomen comics had read about Empedocles 5th-century BCE theory of eyesight.

Depending on your background, you may have developed your sight to include such phenomena as the auras around people's bodies. Or you may have developed skills for seeing and tracking animals in the forest. We each have unique skill sets that we can bring to our dowsing, so consider what you already have and make use of it to improve your accuracy.

Multi-Dimensional Sight

When I look at a location or building where I want to dowse, I turn on a very special inner sight. Using this way of seeing makes the tree, rock, building, or whatever I'm looking at appear to me to glow more vividly, with sharply defined edges. It's like I turned up the contrast on my internal camera. I can't say exactly how I do this, but I sometimes imagine that I'm using my third eye (pineal gland) as an augmented viewer. I allow my "internal lantern" to shine out and meet the object in space, much as Empedocles described.

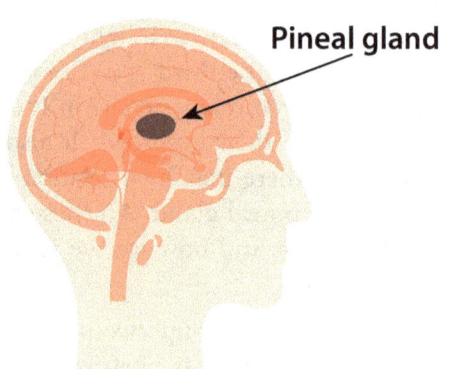

Give it a try and see if you can make this happen for you. It requires you to go to your Dowsing Mind and imagine seeing out from your pineal gland. Don't get tense about trying to make this happen or it won't. Relaxing and breathing deeply and rhythmically may help. Once you accomplish this, it will seem quite natural, and you will wonder why you haven't seen it before. If you have used recreational drugs, you may have experienced this way of seeing while you were high, but you can do it without the aid of chemicals. We say you are seeing into the multi-dimensional realm. If you find this impossible to do, just fake it until you make it. I guarantee that it will come to you.

If you have been seriously practicing all the previous experiments, you may have experienced multi-dimensional sight already. You may recognize this from my description above, or you may have had different sensations. You will know it if you have experienced it, so develop this way of seeing and your dowsing will continue to improve.

Extrasensory Perception

What I'm describing as Dowsing Mind is called extrasensory perception. Look up extrasensory perception in Wikipedia and you will read: "Extrasensory perception or ESP, also called the sixth sense, includes claimed reception of information not gained through the recognized physical senses but sensed with the mind." Now I ask you, what is dowsing? It is extrasensory perception, isn't it! Everything we have been doing so far in this book is extrasensory perception. Also notice that in the Wikipedia definition, ESP is "claimed reception of information . . ." There you have the Establishment view in a nutshell. The Establishment implies that ESP is all a fraud. It doesn't exist. Well, you and I both know that that is one big lie. We experience ESP all the time, and you have been experiencing it in all the dowsing experiments you have been doing.

Story Time

I have several stories to tell you at this point. The first concerns Elyn's mother, Lily, who was quite psychic but refused to admit it. She and Elyn's father took a freighter trip to South America, and they put into port at Lima, Peru, a city they had never visited and knew nothing about. Elyn's mother and father got off the ship, and Lily pointed to one of the public busses that was waiting to pick up passengers from the ship. "We'll take that one," she said. Getting on the bus, they rode into downtown Lima. Then she said, "We're getting off here."

Lily headed straight into a souvenir shop and walked to the back. She went downstairs. In the back was a storage room behind a curtain. Entering the storage room, she pulled a box from under a table and began sorting through the contents, picking out a collection of small ceramic figurines and beaded cords. She took them up to the check-out counter and negotiated a price. From there they went to the local archeology museum and asked one of the staff to identify the objects. All but one of the pieces were authentic pre-Columbian artifacts. When asked how she knew to go to that shop, Lily just giggled and said, "I just knew." Now, that's ESP at work!

"A hallmark of Albert Einstein's career was his use of visualized thought experiments (German: *Gedankenexperiment*) as a fundamental tool for understanding physical issues and for elucidating his concepts to others. Einstein's thought experiments took diverse forms. In his youth, he mentally chased beams of light. . . . For general relativity, he considered a person falling off a roof, accelerating elevators, blind beetles crawling on curved surfaces and the like. . . . In a profound contribution to the literature on quantum mechanics, Einstein considered two particles briefly interacting and then flying apart so that their states are correlated, anticipating the phenomenon known as quantum entanglement." (Wikipedia: "Einstein's thought experiments")

Was Einstein using ESP in his work as a physicist?

Here is another example. Elyn and I were expecting a visit from Elyn's son and family. They got a late start from their home in California and were going to arrive sometime in the middle of the night. We told them to call when they arrived so we could let them in to our rented Airbnb in Arizona. In the middle of the night I suddenly awoke and thought, "they must be here." I got up and looked out, but there was no car. I decided to get a drink of water and go back to bed. Just before getting into bed I thought I would take one more look. Sure enough, there was a car stopped on the street in front of our house. It was them. I got my robe on and opened the door and waved them in. Coincidence? Synchronicity? ESP? You be the judge.

In the Celtic lands such as Ireland and Scotland, there is a phenomenon called *an dara sealladh* or "second sight" that allows individuals who possess it to know future events or see events that are occurring far away. This gift is considered to be hereditary and runs in families, but I think it more likely that some families encourage the development of second sight. *An dara sealladh* is certainly a form of ESP with a long history. Our multi-dimensional sight is similar to *an dara sealladh,* and I know that it can be developed with practice.

Frequencies of Reality

In her book *Hands of Light,* Barbara Ann Brennan speaks at length about what she calls "frequencies of reality," which resemble what I have been calling the multi-dimensional realms. The following quotation is from the section on "The Human Energy Field":

> "Each of the layers above the third is an entire layer of reality with beings, form, and personal functions that go beyond what we normally call human. Each is an entire world in which we live and have our being. Most of us experience these realities during sleep but do not remember them. Some of us can go into those states of reality by expanding the consciousness through meditative techniques. These meditative techniques open the seals between the roots of the chakra layers and thus provide a doorway for consciousness to travel" (Brennan, *Hands of Light: A Guide to Healing Through the Human Energy Field,* 1988, p. 51).

To this I say a hearty "yes!" I have lived most of my adult life there, and I hope you are enjoying your visits there too. The imaginal realm is where the impossible and improbable become the possible and probable.

What does all this have to do with dowsing? After all, dowsers are mostly concerned with identifying things in the 3-D world, not exploring multi-dimensional realms. My experience tells me that my lifetime of work in these realms has enabled me to become a successful dowser. There is an multi-dimensional component that is associated with many of the objects in this plane, and my work in the multi-dimensional realms has enabled me to sense that component more easily.

"Going Multi-Dimensional"

As I said earlier, the imaginal realm is a place we all visit every night. In fact, the area between waking and sleeping (the hypnogogic state) is very much like the state I am in when I am dowsing. I have promised you some exercises using the hypnogogic state. Here are three:

Experiment #11: X-ray Vision

Equipment: your imagination.

Goal: blending the imaginal and the 3-D realms.

If you imagine you are Superman or Superwoman flipping that internal switch, you may get the feel for what "viewing the multi-dimensional" is like. However, instead of seeing the interior of others' bodies, you are seeing the essential energetic nature of the objects around you. For example, when standing stones have been properly oriented to the magnetic lines of the Earthfield, they radiate an energy that looks like faint wisps of smoke. You can see that energy if you are viewing from a multi-dimensional perspective.

Another approach is to imagine you are going to sleep and you are drifting between awake and asleep in that hypnogogic state where the external (3-D) realm dissolves. Now, instead of going to sleep, gently open your eyes a little and look at the world around you. Try to maintain that hypnogogic state with your eyes open. The world will have a different appearance from its normal 3-D appearance.

A third approach is to imagine you are seeing with your third eye. Keep your normal (3-D) eyes open but concentrate on the third eye or pineal gland. The images you will see will look different from their usual appearance.

Try all of these methods and practice the one that comes most naturally to you. Or shift among all three to get a feel for multi-dimensional sight. Here are three more hypnogogic exercises:

Experiment #12: Another Hypnogogic Exercise

Equipment: a candle.

Goal: developing multi-dimensional sight.

Here's a night-time hypnogogic exercise for you. Choose a night when you won't have to get up and go to work in the morning. Prepare for bed in your usual way, but before going to sleep, light a candle beside the bed. Now allow yourself to slip into that dreamy, sliding-down sleepy place with your eyes closed. You know the one. You do it every night. However, this time just open your eyes for a second or so and let the candle flame come to you. Don't do your usual "now I'm going to look at the candle" thing. Just let your eyes gradually open while maintaining that dreamy feeling. Close your eyes again, and once you are back in the hypnogogic state, allow them to open again. See if you can maintain that dreamy in-between state with your eyes open. You may be looking into a multi-dimensional aspect of this realm. Get used to it. It is the doorway into the imaginal realm.

What do you see? How does the candle look? Be sure to blow out the candle when you are done.

Experiment #13: A Meditation Exercise

Equipment: a candle.

Goal: developing multi-dimensional sight.

Here is a daytime meditation exercise for you. Prepare to do R. J. Stewart's Stillness Practice (see p. 12). Light a candle and place it before you in your line of sight. Do the practice with your eyes closed, and when you are at the end, allow your eyes to open and take in the candle flame. Do it without changing to "I'm looking" mode. Just open your eyes for a second or so and let them close again. Can you maintain the meditative state with your eyes open? That is an multi-dimensional aspect of this space. Take note of how it looks. How is it different from everyday reality?

Experiment #14: A Night-Time Dream Practice

Equipment: none.

Goal: developing multi-dimensional sight.

Here is a night-time dream practice. Again, choose a night when you won't have to get up and rush around preparing for work or household chores. When you first wake up and before you open your eyes, think back over the night to see if you remember any dreams or fragments of dreams. It doesn't have to be the next Great American Novel—any tiny fragment will do perfectly well. Hold that image in your mind and just allow your eyes to open slightly. Close them, and combine that image with the image from your dream. Open your eyes again and combine the two images. That internal image combines the multi-dimensional space with the 3-D space. Can you create the composite image?

Gentle Warning

I'm sure you know by now what is coming (after all, you do have the second sight!), but I feel the need to state this warning from time to time. If I'm boring you, just skip to the next section. Please do not go into multi-dimensional viewing while driving or operating machinery. It is vital for your safety that you remain in the 3-D state at those times. Also, make sure that your body is in a safe place before "going multi-dimensional." I sometimes feel a bit dizzy when I view the multi-dimensional space, so I position myself so I can keep my body safe in the 3-D realm. Hold on to something if you also feel dizzy.

But Is It Safe out There?

I haven't mentioned before the question of safety in visiting the multi-dimensional and/or imaginal realms. I haven't wanted to dwell on this question for one very good reason: our fear is energy, and it is an energy that anyone or anything of malicious intent will feed upon. It is their primary food in this realm or in any other. So, don't, and I repeat don't, give them your fear.

That being said, I must say that there are those among our fellow human beings who consciously visit the imaginal realms with malicious intent. And there are those who visit with unconscious malicious intent. Then there are those who are not in physical bodies who also have malicious intent. I have met some of these types in my own work in the imaginal realms. They do exist out there. It's like walking in any city at night. There are areas you should avoid (and perhaps areas you should avoid in the day as well as in the night). You can think about the imaginal realms in a similar way. So how can we be safe there? I offer the method of my friend and teacher, Robert Moss, who is a walker between worlds with vastly more experience than my own. Robert opens and closes every, and I do mean EVERY, class session or practice in his trainings with the following invocation:

> "May our doors and gates and paths be open and our doors and gates and paths between the worlds, and may the doors and gates and paths of any who would do us, or those we love, any harm be closed. May it be so."

I have found this invocation to be highly effective and protective, and I offer it to you and much gratitude to Robert Moss. I urge you to make liberal use of it as we move deeper into the imaginal realms. I will be reminding you from time to time to repeat it. May we all be safe there. May it be so.

Part Three

Even Deeper

"In the beginning was the Word, and the Word was with God, and the Word was God."[6]

What is "the Word?" Well, it wasn't something written on a piece of paper or even carved on stone. Human language, paper, and stone didn't even exist. Remember, this was the very beginning of everything. The word was a sound. What is sound? Vibration. So, God is vibration.

"Everything in life is vibration." – Albert Einstein

There you have it. From the wisdom of Albert Einstein to the King James Bible, everything is vibration—and vibration is energy. I am just a nexus of energy and so are you. The entire 3-D universe is just energy, and so are the multi-dimensional realms. They coexist along with or within God. I can't get my head around that when I'm in the 3-D world, but it becomes obvious when I'm in the multi-dimensional (imaginal) realms.

If I am just energy, I should be able to direct my energy in any way I choose and combine it with the energy that appears to be another object in my space. When I am in the Dowsing Mind, I find that I can do just that, and I say I harmonize myself with this other object. Perhaps I say that because I'm a long-time musician.

---

6   John 1:1, King James Version.

An Appeal to Conscience

As we move ever-deeper into the imaginal realms, I urge you to consider carefully your motivations for taking on these new skills. Please consult your conscience and maintain only the most positive intent as you move in these areas. If you do so, you can be a positive force for good in this troubled world we live in. In fact, it may only be the riches that you and others bring back from the multi-dimensional realms that will save our species. I am completely serious when I make these statements.

Resonance

Imagine yourself sitting at a piano. A *real* upright or grand piano, not a digital one. Press the pedal on the right, which frees up all the strings inside the piano, and sing a single note into the piano. You will hear the piano respond with a ghostly echo of your own voice. Your vocal sound is a vibration, and it travels into the piano and sets some of the strings in motion. This is what is called resonance. In scientific terms, resonance is "The reinforcement or prolongation of sound by reflection from a surface or by the synchronous vibration of a neighboring object."

Another analogy for resonance leads more easily to practical dowsing application. Consider that the site you are going to dowse is like a radio or TV station that is broadcasting a signal at a certain frequency. You, as a dowser, can tune into that signal if you can adjust your own "instrument" to the frequency of the station. You have to be able to tune yourself to a range of frequencies to sense the signal from the station. Going to your Dowsing Mind will help you get there. When you find the right frequency, you can resonate with the signal from the station. Just imagine it and you will be tuned in.

If the site you are going to dowse is the equivalent of a low-power station, you may need to be quite close to it to sense the signal. But if it is a powerful broadcasting station, you can sense the signal from farther away. When I am approaching a very powerful site like a cathedral or a stone circle, I can begin to pick up the signal from a mile or more away. If I know what it looks like, I visualize the site I'm approaching and tune in to its signal. In this way I can already be prepared when I actually arrive at the site.

Now let's return to the idea of multi-dimensional sight. When I'm dowsing or about to enter a sacred site, I look at the object, the building, the rock, or the tree using multi-dimensional sight and I try to harmonize with it. That is, I try to shift my vibration to resonate with the energy of the place or thing. I sometimes say that I am the piano with the right pedal down, and the place I'm looking at is the sound coming in. Or I say that I'm a radio that is tuned to the signal put out by the site. I turn my imaginary internal dial to eliminate the static and get a clear signal. Or say that I am resonating with it. It really works, but you have to try it to believe it. This is an important advanced technique that will improve your dowsing, so I recommend that you start practicing it now.

Experiment #15: Tuning the Instrument

Equipment needed: your multi-dimensional sight.

Goal: harmonizing with a building or object.

Choose an object and shift into multi-dimensional mode. Sense the vibration coming from the object, and shift your vibration to align with it. Go to your Dowsing Mind and imagine that you are tuning that internal dial. This will take considerable practice, so don't expect to achieve it immediately. If the object you are trying to harmonize with is a building, you may find it helpful to place your right hand on the door frame and wait until you feel "at one" with the building. When you are harmonized with the building, you will sense it in the depths of your being. Your dowsing will be more accurate because you are responding from that harmonized place.

Harmonizing on a Grand Scale: The Walkabout

Throughout this book I have periodically talked about Elyn's and my journey following Elen of the Ways across Wales, Ireland, and Scotland. Now that I've explained these new concepts of harmonizing and resonance, I can give you a fuller picture.

As we began to harmonize with the places we were visiting in Wales and with the concept of the trip that was unfolding intuitively rather than being planned, we began to notice signs and symbols that indicated what we were to do next. We were looking for and finding "sidewalk oracles."

For example, we arrived at the Celtic Royal Hotel in Caernarfon in the far north of Wales. We had followed as many of the Sarn Helen ways as we could as we traveled from south Wales to north Wales with our guide, Ros. We were wondering if Caernarfon was the end of our journey and, perhaps, we should then return home to Spain.

After saying goodbye to Ros, we decided to take a walk to familiarize ourselves with the town. Imagine our surprise when we came to a large map and placard painted on a wall labeled "Road St. Helen" (a Christianized version Sarn Helen). It turns out that in the 4th-century CE, Elen, the daughter of the Roman-British ruler Eudal Hen (Octavius), became the wife of Magnus Maximus, the Emperor of the Western part of the Roman Empire from 383 to 388. According to the legend, Elen ordered the construction of the Sarn Helen network to link the north and south of Wales. Her name, Elen, was later anglicized as Helen. And she and Magnus Maximus lived in Segontium, the Roman fortress on the hillside above the town of Caernarfon. What a perfect climax to our trip. We spent the next day visiting the ruins of Segontium in appreciation for the guidance we'd received from Elen of the Ways. But where to go next?

Segontium above Caernarfon, Wales, the legendary home of Helen and Magnus Maximus.

Returning to the hotel that night, Elyn (always the doubter) commented that she hoped this trip hadn't turned into a wild goose chase. Suddenly we realized that this was the key we needed to find the next step of our way. We muscle-tested to find our next destination and got "Ireland." Elyn thought it might be interesting to revisit Killarney National Park in the south of Ireland, but we muscle-tested and got a clear "no." A wild goose chase in Ireland? Hmm, what did that mean?

In the middle of the night, Elyn suddenly awoke with the question: Didn't W. B. Yeats—a favorite poet of Elyn's—write about wild geese? Indeed he did, in "September 1913." His poem "Wild Swans at Coole," in which he writes of wild swans—not geese—also came to mind. We were conflating these two poems, but that didn't stop us from seeing this as a viable sidewalk oracle. Now we knew our goal in Ireland: a visit to the wild swans in Coole Park on the west coast of Ireland.

I opened the Rome2Rio app on my cell phone and found that we could take a bus from Caernarfon to nearby Banger, then a short train ride to Holyhead, followed by a ferry to Dublin. How convenient. That completed our plans for the near future: a bus, train, and ferry journey to Dublin to begin our wild goose chase to Coole Park, with W. B. Yeats as our guide. It was our happy delusion that Elen of the Ways was handing us over to Yeats for the next part of the journey.

Elyn in Yeats's study in Thoor Ballylee, near Coole Park

While we were in Dublin, we visited the W. B. Yeats permanent exhibition at the National Library of Ireland. When we walked into the exhibition, we were greeted by a recording of "Wild Swans at Coole," which we took as a confirmation of our sidewalk oracle. The recorded loop included many other poems, so it was synchronistic that the "Wild Swans" was playing at that moment. When we were visiting Coole Parke, we noticed The Deer Pen, which is home to a herd of red deer. We took that as an indication that Elen of the Ways was with us still.

Notice how we were resonating with the subtle messages we were receiving. A chance phrase (wild goose chase) suggested other ideas (didn't Yeats write about wild geese?), which gradually coalesced (aided by a search on Rome2Rio) into a plan for the immediate future. This is how we made our plans on our grand walkabout. And this is how I was learning about the power of letting things unfold spontaneously. We were living our lives by synchronicity and enjoying the surprises that continually revealed themselves.

The appearance of Elen of the Ways on the magazine cover in Edinburgh airport (see pp. 65-66) erased any doubt in our minds that we were being guided by Elen of the Ways. That freed us to experience an enjoyable adventure filled with unexpected pleasures. When we traveled looking out for the next sign, we found ourselves relating differently with the land and the people around us. Each day was filled with meaningful events. Sometimes it was the appearance of a tree in the woods that resembled an antlered deer, sometimes we would suddenly notice trophy stag heads on the wall in a café we were visiting for coffee. We also found that the trip flowed more smoothly than our usual adventures. We said that we were "in the flow" of events. In other words, we were in resonance.

Elen of the Ways showing up in the forest

Just when the next step would look problematic, we would find an unexpected solution that would not only solve the problem but would be fun as well. Not having a set itinerary gave us the freedom to shift plans at a moment's notice, and we did so regularly. The only downside to this mode of travel was that it tended to be much more expensive (and by its very nature, more uncertain) than reserved-in-advance itineraries. The compensation was that when a unique opportunity showed up, we could follow it without the hassle of changing already made reservations.

We called our new travel strategy a "walkabout" after the Indigenous Australians' way of walking the land. We decided to live the rest of our lives as a walkabout as much as possible. Whenever people ask us what our plans are, we respond that we no longer make plans. The most we do is have intentions, but they can change at a moment's notice.

What does all this have to do with dowsing? Everything. Living a life of planning is living totally in the 3-D world. It is all left brain. Living life as a walkabout allows the intuitive senses to guide you, which is exactly what you do when you dowse. Living spontaneously increases our ability to harmonize with the places we visit and increases my accuracy with dowsing. I can recommend this way of being in the world without reservation.

I know that being retired and not having a set work schedule makes it much easier for me to live my life as a walkabout. But even if you have a 9-to-5 job, you will benefit from allowing your intuitive senses to inform your work. And you can make the other parts of your life more spontaneous. I predict that you will find it enjoyable, and you will improve your dowsing skills at the same time. Whether you are noticing meaningful events or bringing meaning to the events of your life, you will find your life much more satisfying.

Experiment #16: Experiencing a Walkabout

Equipment needed: a sense of adventure and some travel gear.

Goal: practice in noticing sidewalk oracles.

Are you ready to try something really wild? Here is a one- or two-day exercise that can give you a feel for what our walkabout in Wales, Ireland, and Scotland was like. Ready? Let's go!

Select two or three places that are easy for you to get to and you would like to explore further. Now, muscle-test to pick one of them. You know the routine. You get ready to test muscle strength in one of the three ways I suggested (with an assistant testing your arm, with linked fingers, or with the second finger pushing the first). Then pick one of the places and ask, "Is it in my highest interest to do the walkabout at . . . ?" One will probably show up as a "yes," or you may need to look for another locale. You can also ask a series of questions like: "On a scale of 1 to 10, with 10 being the highest, it is in my highest interest to experience a walkabout at . . . (location)." Of course, you can use your rods or a pendulum to make the selection instead. You have a number of options for dowsing your answers at this point. Do what feels most comfortable to you.

When you have a site picked out, decide if you are going to spend one day or two with the exercise. If you decide on two days, you will need to think about where you are going to sleep the first night. And, by the way, you can share this adventure with a friend if they are totally clued in with what you are doing and willing to let go and just go along with the process.

So, now you are there. Go into Dowsing Mind mode and harmonize with the place. Notice anything that catches your attention. It may be something you have seen before, or it may be something you haven't noticed. These are Robert Moss's "sidewalk oracles." For example, it may be a bird call, a phrase in an advertisement at the train station, part of a sentence you overhear from a passerby, a person you meet on the street, or anything else that grabs your attention.

Ask yourself, "What is the message for me here?" or "What is this trying to tell me?" Wait for an answer to appear. Your left brain may try to jump in and suggest an answer. Be patient and let the answer unfold. When you have an answer, ask, "What is this telling me to do next?" If it is possible, do what it tells you to do. If impossible, ask, "Give me another answer."

When you arrive at the next spot, repeat the same process. Keep on repeating this process, taking time to be at each place long enough to absorb its vibe. Make notes about your observations or keep a journal if you prefer. Take time to eat and have some refreshments in the process. When your allotted time is over, return home and write up a short narrative about the experience. Include observations about how the walkabout made you feel.

If the walkabout above seems too much for you, you can easily do a scaled-down version by taking an hour-long walkabout in your neighborhood. It can be quite informative, and it may encourage you to do the more extended version. Maybe someday you will even try a month-long walkabout like our trip with Elen of the Ways.

Was that fun? I hope so. Maybe it will encourage you to live more of your life as a walkabout. Also notice that this experiment gave you many opportunities to practice your dowsing skills.

The Prevailing Fantasy

There is a prevailing fantasy that this material world is all there is. It is called materialism or, sometimes, physicalism. There was a good reason that it arose. Before the rise of modern science, this material realm (the 3-D realm) was little understood. In Europe, the (Catholic) Church controlled people's lives and their thoughts, and the material realm was denigrated. As the power of the Church diminished and science and technology successfully remade Western society, the fantasy arose that the material realm is all there is.

Scientific materialists debunk anything they can't measure rather than realizing their equipment is technologically limited. It is somewhat like a color-blind person proclaiming that the colors red and green simply don't exist. This situation has resulted in an utter disregard for the multi-dimensional realm. They think it's a fantasy. We are now living with the misguided notion that science and technology will solve all our problems and answer all our questions if we just keep trying. So far, this has proven to be the *real* fantasy.

Part Four

The Problem of Consciousness

A problem that has plagued science is that it has been unable to explain consciousness. It attempts to do so by claiming that consciousness is just an epiphenomenon of our brain activity. But evidence continues to accumulate that this is not the case. This consciousness, which all humans share, continues to elude scientists. The solution is to realize that scientific materialism is just plain wrong, and consciousness, not matter, is fundamental. Matter develops out of consciousness, which implies that all matter must have consciousness to one degree or another.

So, here is my preferred cutting-edge Theory of Everything (TOE): the 3-D realm, the multi-dimensional realms, and consciousness are all simply vibration, as is the whole multiverse, including Divinity. As a life-long musician, I would say that I'm just a song, and so are you, and so is everything else. Enjoy the great symphony that we are creating together! I hope you are finding it harmonious and enjoyable.

What I hope you have learned from all our dowsing exercises is that your consciousness is more powerful and far reaching than you had imagined, and it bridges the 3-D and multi-dimensional realms.

If you want to pursue the idea that everything is vibration, I recommend *The World is Sound—Nada Brahma* by Joachim-Ernst Berendt (Berendt, 1983). This long excursion into music and the landscape of consciousness goes in depth into this concept, using music as its principal metaphor. Reading it will expand your understanding of the universe as vibration. You will come back from these realms a much better dowser and a more grounded human being.

If you prefer a more scientific approach, then read *The Intelligence of the Cosmos* by Ervin Laszlo. At the outset Laszlo states, "In the new concept, the things that furnish the world are not pieces of matter. Surprisingly (or perhaps not so surprisingly, because this has been an age-old intuition) they are basically vibration" (Laszlo, 2017, p. 11).

Subjective Space – Map Dowsing

Map dowsing is an intangible form of dowsing that can often be corroborated on the land. This will be a shorter section than others because I have less experience with it than with the other forms we've been discussing. For a much more complete treatment of the subject, I refer you to Elizabeth Brown's *Dowsing: The Ultimate Guide for the 21st Century* (Brown, 2010).

A common proverb states that the "map is not the territory." In map dowsing it is important to change your belief in that proverb and realize that the map is, indeed, the territory—or at the least, a good representation of the territory. If you can believe this proposition, you can dowse the map as if it were the location you want to dowse but cannot reach for one reason or another. Map dowsers use their skills to dowse for faults, energy lines, and anything you might dowse for on the land—including a good place to relocate to or travel to. We used map dowsing to determine some of the places to visit on our Elen of the Ways walkabout.

To practice map dowsing, take out a map of an area that you want to know more about. The more detailed the map and the higher the resolution the better. I prefer ordinance survey and topographic maps that give me visual information about the terrain. Most map dowsers find that the pendulum is a better tool for map dowsing than the rods, so take out your favorite pendulum.

Form a clear picture in your mind of the territory in question, and tell yourself that you are looking at the actual territory. Enter into the Dowsing Mind, remembering to perform all the preparatory steps you routinely use when dowsing. Now ask the pendulum to show you where on the map the features you want to identify are located. Move the pendulum over the map until you get a strong hit on one location. Make a note of that location and have it confirmed by field dowsing if possible.

Map dowsing

Remember:

- Check to see if your internal energetic system is in balance. Rebalance if necessary.
- Ask permission (Am I connected to Highest Source? May I, can I, and should I ask these questions?).
- State what you are seeking in clear, unambiguous terms.
- Go to your Dowsing Mind and shift your state of awareness.
- Place the pendulum in search position.
- Begin dowsing over the map.
- When you get an indication that you have found what you are looking for, double-check by dowsing across the map from a different direction.

If you find this a reliable way of working, you are well on your way to becoming a map dowser. If the idea of map dowsing strains your credibility, I would strongly recommend Elizabeth Brown's book. She presents much information about this technique that may help you get over your skepticism.

Dowsing for Health

I have presented a number of ways that dowsing can improve your health by helping you make better life choices. Another way that dowsing can impact your health is through diagnosis of health issues and identification of potential treatments. Over the years, we have consulted a number of health-care professionals who used muscle-testing and dowsing, including medical intuitive Elizabeth Brown, acupuncturist Ferran Blasco-Aguasca, and my daughter and Pranic healer, Stephanie Crystaal. (See p. 115 for more information.)

Subjective Time

In my youth there was a popular comic strip called Alley Oop, in which a 20th-century scientist named Dr. Wonmug invented a time machine and brought a cave man named Alley Oop and some of his friends from the prehistoric past into the present time. The strip continues to be published to this day. What we experience in dowsing is a form of time travel every bit as mysterious as that experienced by Alley Oop. We call this time "subjective time" as opposed to clock time, and our dowsing all takes place there.

If this seems too far-fetched and "woo-woo" for you, consider an experience I just had. I was online using an app called "Go to Meeting" to meet with 25 other people for a group meditation. The people in this group were in all the time zones in the US and Europe and as far away as Israel. We were meditating on stopping time, space, and movement. In another room in our house, Elyn was on another app with another group that was gathered together from at least as many time zones and diverse locations around the world. It was nighttime for some, noon for others, and morning the next day for at least one participant. Meanwhile, my neighbor across the street was in her front yard visiting with another of our neighbors. I'm sure she had no concept of the multiple variants in time and space that were going on just across the street.

I suggest that we are usually a lot like my neighbor in thinking that we are "here and now." The experience we were having just across the street was much more time and space fluid. As dowsers, we get used to this more fluid time and space. It is the time and space we work in.

Does All Matter Have Consciousness?

The so-called "hard problem of consciousness" that has plagued science and appears to have no solution is bringing an ancient philosophy called pan-psychism back into contemporary thought. To quote Wikipedia, "In philosophy of mind, pan-psychism is the view that mind or a mind-like aspect is a fundamental and ubiquitous feature of reality." In other words, all matter has at least a modicum of consciousness.

An alternative explanation to account for the hard problem of consciousness was proposed by MIT professor Max Tegmark. He proposes that there may be a hitherto unknown state of matter that he calls "perceptronium." This is a state of matter that, in itself, has consciousness.

Pan-psychism or perceptronium are plausible explanations for the experience I have called "harmonizing" with a site I am dowsing. I believe that when I harmonize with a place, my consciousness is making contact with the consciousness of the place I'm dowsing. The experience of heightened reality I have described when I go into Dowsing Mind is my consciousness resonating vibrationally with the vibrational consciousness of the place. That the place looks more radiant and clearer is the way my physical senses respond to my harmonizing with the site. One could say I "see" it more like it actually is: vibration.

Of course, as is so often the case, science is only coming around to a truth that mystics and shamans have known for centuries. Native Americans, for example, have long recognized that the "plant nations" and "stone nations" possess consciousness. They talk about the spirit of a plant or a stone as "a being" that they can communicate with like they communicate with other conscious beings. Such personification has the advantage that it makes communication in the multi-dimensional realms feel quite natural. If personification helps you to become familiar with the reality of the multi-dimensional realms, by all means see the places you are dowsing as beings with consciousness. Anything that helps you to sense the reality of the multi-dimensional realm is good.

Experiment #17: Making Friends[7] with Plants and Stones

Equipment needed: a favorite plant, tree, or stone.

Goal: befriending other conscious beings.

For this exercise you will need to select a favorite plant, tree, or stone to develop a relationship with. I have a

---

[7] "Friends" is, of course, a very humanocentric way to describe establishing a positive, reciprocal relationship with a plant or stone.

favorite old cottonwood tree near my home in Arizona that I call Grandmother Cottonwood. I visit this tree regularly and have extended conversations with her. I don't see her in near-human terms, but when I visit her and go into Dowsing Mind, the tree has a glowing "presence." That she is an ancient being is obvious, and I feel that I get excellent advice and counsel whenever I go to her. I was sitting at her base on a beautiful Sunday afternoon recently, and she asked me to quote her in this book. Here is her statement, word for word: "Your 'hard problem of consciousness' is not a hard problem for me at all." Thank you, Grandmother Cottonwood!

Grandmother Cottonwood

Select a tree or a stone that has a glowing presence to you in your Dowsing Mind. Remember that ancient trees and stones are vastly older than you are. They have accumulated much wisdom to share with you. Go to the one you want to establish a relationship with. Go into your Dowsing Mind and ask him/her/it to be your "friend." You don't need to speak your request aloud. Ask in your thoughts with the secure knowledge that you will be heard. Ask what you can bring as an offering when you visit. In the desert southwest of the USA, offerings are usually corn meal, sage, or other natural products of the land. If you are in different climes, the offering may be something native to your region, like oat cakes and mead. Quiet your mind and wait patiently for your new friend to respond to you. If you don't get any response after several minutes, ask again. And ask a third time. There is a saying that asking three times shows how sincere you are. If you don't get a response after three times, you may need to return another time or select a different being to be your friend. When you get a positive response, you will have an internal knowing that the connection has been made. Be sure that you have the proper offering available for the next time you visit.

When you have that internal knowing of connection, you can have a conversation and ask questions of your new friend. Questions about your dowsing would be good subjects of conversation, as are questions about what you can manifest on the 3-D plane on behalf of your new friend. Remember that bringing back riches into the 3-D plane from the multi-dimensional realms is what separates being an imaginaut from being a daydreamer. Ask many questions and wait patiently for answers to come to you. This is the way these conversations in the multi-dimensional realm go. When your conversation is over, say goodbye and thank your new friend for taking time to be with you. That would be a good time to give your friend another offering.

The Scope of the Multi-Dimensional Realms

We are nearing the end of this brief introduction to the multi-dimensional realms. My chosen entry point was dowsing, but we have moved far beyond that to explore a universe far greater than this 3-D universe we think we live in. You have just made contact with another conscious, living being in the form of a tree or stone. Take a look around you at this 3-D realm and consider that every part of this realm is conscious and living. The extent of this multi-dimensional universe is vastly greater than the 3-D realm—a realm our astronauts have barely begun to explore. Scientists have just begun to imagine that the multi-dimensional realm might exist and have not, as yet, been able to develop tools to explore it. The mystics, imaginauts, shamans, and other explorers of the multi-dimensional universe have been out there for millennia, and they have only begun to explore the expanse of this place.

A Spiritual Practice

Here is a practice that I do nearly every day of my life. It is from Terry Patten, one of my many teachers. I say aloud:

"Notice the mystery,

How everything is,

But no one knows what it really is.

Feel the mystery.

Breathe the mystery.

Be the mystery."

I have been repeating this practice daily for more than ten years, and it continues to become more profound every day. As I have deepened my experience with the multi-dimensional realms, Patten's practice opens up areas for me that I could not have imagined before. The 3-D realm is no less mysterious, but the multi-dimensional realms just keep expanding in mystery. There appears to be no end there, and I don't expect I will have begun to explore the depths of the multi-dimensional realms in this lifetime. Try the practice for yourself and see where it takes you.

At the risk of spoiling the beauty of Terry Patten's practice, I will say a few more things about the final three statements.

"Feel the mystery." Feeling takes me immediately beyond the realm of the left brain. I'm not just thinking about the mystery, I'm feeling it. That is a completely different way of approaching the subject.

"Breathe the mystery." Breathing the mystery takes it even more deeply into the depths of my being. As my acupuncturist/geomancer friend Ferran Blasco-Aguasca says, "Nothing is more fundamental to living and healing than breathing. Food, clothing, relationships, money, fame, and everything in our lives are secondary to breathing. Simply put: no breathing, game over" (Blasco-Aguasca, *Healing Now: A Path to Oprtimal Well-Being and Self-Love Through Healing Meditation,* 2020, p. 19).

"Be the mystery." This, to me, is the ultimate truth—*I am the mystery.* My consciousness is mysterious beyond any imagining of it. This is the realm of becoming one with everything. There is no duality here. All is Oneness. And all is mystery.

This is where our journey into the multi-dimensional realms takes us—to ultimate unity with everything.

Bringing It Back to the 3-D Realm

As I have said multiple times in this book, our task as humans living in this 3-D realm is to bring some of the riches of the multi-dimensional realms back into manifestation here in this realm. If we fail to do so, we are only day-dreamers playing around in alternative realities. The book you are now reading is a document that I brought through from the multi-dimensional realm. It came as a series of "downloads" during my dreamtime. I got up each morning and entered them into my computer. Sometimes, I would also take a nap in the daytime and get another download. Of course, the original version that came through in dreams was edited and expanded several times with the assistance of my wife, editor, and fellow imaginaut, Elyn Aviva. We passed several versions of the manuscript back and forth and shaped it into the form you are now reading.

There are many techniques for entering the imaginal realm and manifesting the results in this realm. I can only tell you some of those that I have found. I encourage you to try my techniques and then develop some of your own. Read what other imaginauts, like Albert Einstein, Robert Moss, Henri Corbin, Cynthia Bourgeault, Sharon Blackie, Veronica Goodchild, etc. (see p. 114) have said about how they work, and expand your own horizons.

Conclusion

We are now approaching the end of this book. As I said at the beginning, I have tried to lead you deeply into your innermost being to awaken senses that you might not have known you have. It was my goal to lead you gently from the agreed-upon (3-D) reality into the depths and heights of the multi-dimensional realms. I hope the ride has been enjoyable, and you are growing more comfortable with these alternate realities. You may be curious to know how others have practiced the dowsing art, and I encourage you to explore further.

One of my first dowsing teachers was Sig Lonegren, who wrote the classic *Spiritual Dowsing: Tools for Exploring the Intangible Realms* (Gothic Image, 2007). Sig presents a very logical and well-thought-through introduction to dowsing as it was practiced in much of the 20th century. There are many nuts-and-bolts details there. My personal approach to dowsing techniques is not as doctrinaire as Sig's, but you can't go wrong trying out his step-by-step instructions, even though you may choose to continue to use the techniques you have developed with this book. As a classic introduction to the subject there is no better than Sig's, in my opinion.

Throughout this book I have referred to Elizabeth Brown's *Dowsing: The Ultimate Guide for the 21st Century.* Her book is the most complete guide to dowsing that I know of. Elizabeth has documented many scientific studies of dowsing and the intuitive senses. She will dispel any suspicions of "woo-woo" that you may still harbor. I keep her book on my shelf and refer to it often. I recommend that you do so as well.

It is important that you continue to practice your dowsing techniques and find out what works for you. I have my own habits, which I have detailed in this book, but you must make dowsing your own by trying out new techniques and asking what skills you already possess that will enhance your dowsing. I have used my professional background in music and my curiosity about the science of sound to develop my personal approach to dowsing. What skills have you developed that you can use in a similar way? Give this some thought, and I'll bet you can think of things to incorporate into your dowsing repertoire.

I'm very curious to know what your experiences are as you continue to develop your skills. With this in mind, I've created a Facebook group called The Dowsing Mind, which I invite you to join. Just log on to Facebook and enter the search words, "The Dowsing Mind." When you arrive at the site, enter "read your book" in the blank provided and I'll welcome you to the club. Here you will find others who are exploring the art and maybe even pick up some valuable hints. It is also a place to share your own experiences with a small but growing group of fellow explorers. I'll be checking in to see what is happening and to share experiences.

Bon voyage and happy travels!

Additional Resources

National Dowsing Societies

This is a by-no-means exhaustive list of national dowsing societies. If you don't see your country listed below, do a Google search and you may find your national organisation. I have found these organisations welcoming to all newcomers, so don't hesitate to contact your national organisation. There are also regional and local dowsing groups, for example, the Trencrom Dowsers in Cornwall, England (https://www.trencromdowsers.org.uk/).

The British Society of Dowsers

https://britishdowsers.org/

American Society of Dowsers

https://dowsers.org/

The Canadian Society of Dowsers

https://canadiandowsers.org/

The Irish Society of Diviners

https://irishdiviners.com/

West of Scotland Dowsers

http://www.wosd.org.uk/

Italian Society of Dowsers

https://www.airmilano.net/

Dowsers Society of NSW, Inc. (Australia)

http://www.dowsingaustralia.com/

Dowsing Society of Victoria, Inc. (Australia)
http://www.dsv.org.au/index.htm

Association des Amis de la Radiesthésie (France)
http://www.lesamisdelaradiesthesie.fr/

Österreichischer Verband für Radiästhesie & Geobiologie (Austria)
http://www.slagruta.org/inenglish.html

Bibliography

Berendt, Joachim-Ernst. *The World is Sound.* Rochester: Destiny Books, 1983.

Blackie, Sharon. *The Enchanted Life: Unlocking the Magic of the Everyday.* Timberlake: Ambrosia Press, 2018.

Blasco-Aguasca, Ferran. *Healing Now: A Path to Optimal Well-Being and Self-Love Through Healing Meditation.* Rochester: Joyful Heart Institute Publications, 2020.

Bourgeault, Cynthia. *Eye of the Heart: A Spiritual Journey into the Imaginal Realm.* Boulder: Shambhala Publications, 2020.

Brennan, Barbara Ann. *Hands of Light: A Guide to Healing Through the Human Energy Field.* New York: Bantam Books, 1988.

Brown, Elizabeth. *Dowsing: The Ultimate Guide for the 21st Century.* Carlsbad: Hay House, 2010.

Corbin, Henri. *Creative Imagination in the Sufism of Ibn Arabi.* Princeton: Bollingen, 2014.

Goodchild, Veronica. *Songlines of the Soul: Pathways to a New Vision for a New Century.* Lake Worth: Ibis Press, 2012.

Khan, Hazrat Inayat. *The Dance of the Soul: Gayan Vadan Nirtan.* New Delhi: Motillal Banarsidass Publishers, 2007.

Lachman, Gary. *Lost Knowledge of the Imagination.* Edinburgh: Floris Books, 2017.

Laszlo, Ervin. *The Intelligence of the Cosmos: Why Are We Here?* Rochester: Inner Traditions, 2017.

Lonegren, Sig. *Spiritual Dowsing.* Glastonbury: Gothic Image Publications, 1986.

Moss, Robert. *Active Dreaming.* Novato: New World Library, 2011.

Moss, Robert. *Dreamgates.* Novato: New World Library, 1998.

Moss, Robert. *Sidewalk Oracles: Playing with Signs, Symbols, and Synchronicity in Everyday Life.* Novato: New World Library, 2015.

Stewart, R. J. *Earth Light.* Lake Toxaway: Mercury Publishing, 1992.

Links

Sig Lonegren—www.geomancy.org,

    http://www.geomancy.org/index.php/dowsing

Elizabeth Brown—https://www.causativediagnosis.com

Stephanie Crystaal—positiveenergyhealer@yahoo.com

Dominic Susani—https://energeticgeometry.com

Gary White—www.fandangolife.com

    www.pilgrimsprocess.com

    www.powerfulplaces.com

Index

A

Afterlife 73
Akashic records 73
alpha 9, 27
altered state 72
amethyst 42
an dara sealladh 83
auras 6, 79

B

beta 9
blind spring 1
body dowsing 48
Bovis scale 46
brow chakra 79

C

Casablanca 79
clock time 102
Coelbryn 39
computer programming 29
consciousness 11, 12, 28, 31, 32, 37, 38, 69, 72, 73, 74, 83, 99, 103, 104, 108

Coole Park 93, 94
Council of Elders 73
creative artist 77
creative thinker 77

D

daydreamer 76, 77
delta 9
depth of water 30, 63
divining rod 5
dominant hand 14
dowsing chart 45
dreamland 12

E

earth energy lines 6
Elen of the Ways 38, 64, 65, 66, 92, 94, 95, 98, 100
Elizabeth Brown 102, 115
Empedocles 78, 79, 80
ESP 81, 82, 83
Eudal Hen 92
extra-sensory 48
extrasensory perception 81

F

Facebook 112
faeries 30
faery realms 73
fault 6, 31, 34, 35, 36, 38, 52

G

gamma 9
genius 77
geode 42
God 2, 52, 89
Goddess 52
GPS 77
Grandmother Cottonwood 105
Great Spirit 52
grounding 33, 64
ground penetrating radar 22, 26, 33

H

harmonizing 91, 92, 104
Hazrat Inayat Khan 79
Heaven 73
Highest Source 52, 67, 101
Humphery Bogart 79
hypnogogic 74, 84, 85

I

imaginal 4, 12, 73, 74, 76, 84, 85, 87, 88, 89, 90, 109
Indigenous 2, 96
Ingrid Bergman 79
Inner Convocation 73
intangibles 6
intuition 7, 55, 64, 100

K

kinesiology 48

L

Land of Eternal Youth 74
light pollution 1
lucid dream 71

M

Magnus Maximus 92
malicious intent 87
map dowsing 100, 102
materialism 98, 99
meditation 9, 12, 13, 32, 38, 71, 86, 103
Moses 2, 3

multi-dimensional sight 81, 83, 85, 86, 91

muscle testing 5, 48, 50, 55, 56, 62

mystery 11, 107, 108

N

neural oscillations 9

O

Other World 74

P

physicalism 98

physical sensation 47

pineal gland 79, 80, 85

plant nations 104

potable water 1

prevailing fantasy 98

proper dosage 62

pseudoscience 5

psychic 81

R

racism 58

red rock formations 57

resonance 9, 44, 90, 92, 95

R. J. Stewart 12, 75

Robert Moss 11, 56, 64, 71, 73, 76, 87, 88, 109

Rome2Rio 93, 94

S

Sarn Helen 38, 39, 40, 64, 92

search position 14, 15, 23, 26, 27, 32, 34, 35, 37, 67, 101

self-hypnosis 70, 72

self-isolation 60

sensory data 48

sexism 58

sidewalk oracles 56, 64, 65, 92, 97

Sig Lonegren 3, 111, 115, 121

sixth sense 48, 81

spiraling path 69

stone nations 104

subjective time 102

Sufi 11, 79

sweet spot 20, 21, 26

T

theta 9, 11, 27

third eye 79, 80, 85

Tír na nÓg, 74

U

Underworld 73

Universal Consciousness 52

V

vibration 89, 90, 91, 99, 100, 104
visualization 25, 72
Void 13, 52

W

walkabout 57, 60, 94, 96, 97, 98, 100
W. B. Yeats 93, 94
wildcat 28

X

x-ray vision 79

About the Author

After his retirement from Iowa State University as Distinguished Professor of Music, Gary White began what he called his "second life." Although he had composed and published over 50 musical compositions for orchestra, band, chorus, and other ensembles, developed the music theory curriculum for the university and inaugurated the electronic music studio, and authored numerous textbooks on music theory—Gary realized there was a whole wide world out there to explore.

Walking the 500-mile pilgrimage road, the Camino de Santiago, across Spain with his wife, Elyn Aviva, triggered a strong need in him to go deeper. He wanted to better understand the power of place. Gary began a serious study of dowsing, sacred geometry, and geomancy, working with experts such as Dominique Susani, Sig Lonegren, Ferran Blasco, and Anne Parker. He and Elyn began co-authoring a series of guidebooks to powerful places and sacred sites in Europe. This series currently includes: *Powerful Places in Cornwall and the Isles of Scilly, Powerful Places in Wales, Powerful Places in Ireland, Powerful Places in Scotland, Powerful Places in Brittany, Powerful Places on the Caminos de Santiago, Powerful Places in Catalonia,* and *Powerful Places in Malta.*

www.ingramcontent.com/pod-product-compliance
Lightning Source LLC
Chambersburg PA
CBHW070052120426
42742CB00048B/2405